ISLAM
—AND—
PEACE

Presented to ....

From ....

Date ....

ISLAM
— AND —
PEACE

MAULANA WAHIDUDDIN KHAN

Goodword
B·O·O·K·S

Translated by
Dr. Farida Khanam

First published 1999
Reprinted 2000

Dis m .Utributed by
AL-RISALA
The Islamic Centre
1, Nizamuddin West Market,
New Delhi 110 013
Tel. 4625454,4611128
Fax 4697333, 4647980
e-mail: skhan@vsnl.com
website: www.alrisala.org

Printed by Nice Printing Press, Delhi

Contents

PART I

Faith and Reason

In its issue no. 134 (1992), the journal, *Faith and Reason*, published from Manchester College, Oxford (England), brought out an article titled, 'The Relationship between Faith and Reason', by Dr Paul Badham. Paul Badham is a Professor of Theology and Religious Studies at St. David's College, Lampeter, in the University of Wales. His paper in this issue had been presented at a Conference of the Institute of Philosophy of the Russian Academy of Science in Moscow in November 1991.

Professor Badham's paper can indeed be called thought-provoking, and as such, is worth reading, but he has made certain points with which I do not agree. He states that philosophical certainty should not be confused with religious certitude. He writes: 'As a philosopher of religion I feel compelled to acknowledge that faith could never be placed on the same level of certainty as scientific knowledge' (p. 6). On the contrary, I feel that faith and belief can be placed on the same level of certainty as scientific theory. At least, in the twentieth century there is no real difference between the two.

Knowledge is composed of two kinds of things, Bertrand Russell puts it, knowledge of things and knowledge of truths. This dichotomy exists in religion as well as in science. For instance, to the scientist who regards biological evolution as a scientific fact, there are two aspects to be considered. One is related to the organic part of species and the other relates to the law of evolution which is inherently and covertly operative in the continuing process of change among the species.

When an evolutionist studies the outward physical appearance of species, he may be said to be studying 'things'. Whereas when he studies the law of evolution, he deals with that aspect of the subject which is termed the study or knowledge of truths.'

Every evolutionist knows that there does exist a basic difference between the two aspects. As far as the study of things or the phenomena of evolution is concerned, direct evidence is available. For instance, because the study of fossils found in various layers of the earth's crust is possible at the level of observation, working hypothesis may be based thereon.

On the contrary, as far as facts about the law of evolution are concerned, due to the impossibility of objective observation, direct argument is not possible. For instance, the concept of sudden mutations in the organs is entirely based on assumptions rather than on direct observation. In the case of mutations, external changes are observable, but the cause, that is, the law of nature, is totally unobservable. That is why all the evolutionists make use of indirect argument, which in logic is known as inferential argument.

The concept of mutation forms the basis of the theory of evolution. However there are two aspects to the matter.

One comes under observation, but the second part is totally unobservable. It is only by making use of the principle of inference that this second part of evolution may be included in the theory of evolution.

It is a commonplace that all the offspring of men or animals are not uniform. Differences of one kind or another are to be found. In modern times this biological phenomenon has been scientifically studied. These studies have revealed spontaneous changes suddenly produced in the foetus in the mother's womb. It is these changes that are responsible for the differences between children of the same parents.

These differences between offsprings are observable. But the philosophy of evolution subsequently formed on the basis of this observation is totally unobservable and is based only on inferential argument. That is to say that the 'things' of evolution are observable, while the 'truths' inferred from observation are unobservable.

Now, what the evolutionist does is put a goat at one end and a giraffe at the other. Then taking some middle specimens of the fossils he forms a theory that the neck of one of the offspring of the earlier generation of the goat was somewhat taller. Then when this particular offspring with the taller neck gave birth, this tallness for generations over millions of years ultimately converted the initial goat with a taller neck into a species like the giraffe in its advanced stage. Charles Darwins writes of this change in his book *The Origin of Species:* "..it seems to me almost certain that an ordinary hoofed quadruped might be converted into a giraffe" (p. 169).

In this case, the existence of differences between the various offspring of a goat is itself a known fact. But the accumulation of this difference, generation after generation, over millions of years resulting in a new species known as 'giraffe' is wholly unobservable and unrepeatable. This conclusion has been inferred from observation only; the whole process of mutation developing into a new species has never come under our direct observation.

Exactly the same is true of the subject of religion. One aspect of the study of religion is the study of its history, its personalities, its injunctions, its rites and its rituals. The above division (knowledge of things and knowledge of truths) amounts to a study of the 'things' of religion. In respect of religion, objective information is likewise available. As such, the study of religion too can be done on the basis of direct observations exactly as is done in the study of biological evolution.

The second aspect of the study of religion is what is termed, in general, beliefs pertaining to the unseen world. These are the beliefs that are beyond our known sensory world. That is, the existence of God and the angels, revelation, hell and heaven, etc. In this other aspect of religion direct observations do not exist. The study of religion must, therefore, be done in the light of that logical principle called inference on the basis of observation, that is, the same logical principle which the evolutionists employ in the second aspect of their theory.

Looked at in the light of this principle, both religion and science are at a par. Both have two equally different parts. One part is based on such scientific certainty as permits direct argument. The other part is based on scientific inference, to prove which only the principle of indirect argument may be used. Keeping this logical division before us, we can find no actual difference between the two.

The unnecessary apologia for religious uncertainty

made by Professor Badham is occasioned by his inability to consider this difference, and his confusing one area of study with another. Making the error of false analogy, he is comparing the first part of science to the second part of religion and looking at the second part of religion in the light of the first part of science. This meaningless comparison is responsible for the ill-considered conclusions he has arrived at in his article.

Had the worthy Professor compared the first part of science to the first part of religion and the second part of science to the second part of the religion, his inferiority complex (as a man of religion) would have ceased to exist. He would have felt that, purely as a matter of principle the wrong parallels had been drawn. The argument used in the first part of science is equally applicable to the first part of religion. Similarly the argument applied to the second part of science is equally applicable to the second part of religion.

This is a truth which has been acknowledged even by a staunch and leading atheist like Bertrand Russell. At the beginning of his book *Why I am not a Christian* he has set forth what he considers a valid argument. He points out that in his view all the great religions of the world— Buddhism, Hinduism, Christianity, Islam and Communism—were all untrue and harmful, and that it is not possible to prove their validity from the logical point of view. Those who have opted for one religion or the other have done so, according to Russell, under the influence of their traditions and environment, rather than on the strength of argument.

However, Bertrand Russell has admitted this fact when he says, "there is one of these arguments which is not purely logical. I mean the argument from design. This argument, however, was destroyed by Darwin."

He intends here to say that the existence of God is proved by the argument that in his world where there is design, there should be a designer. He admits that this method of argument in its nature is the same as that used to prove scientific concepts. However, even after this admission, he rejects this argument by saying that it has been destroyed by Darwinism.

This is, however, a wholly baseless point, as Darwin's theory is related to the Creator's process of creation rather than to the existence of Creator. To put it briefly, Darwinism states that the various species found in the world were not separate creations but had changed from one species into separate species over a prolonged period of evolution by a process of natural selection.

It is obvious that this theory is not related to the existence or non-existence of God. It deals with the process of Creation instead of the Creator. That is to say, if it was hitherto believed that God created each species separately, now after accepting the theory of evolution it has to be believed that God originally created an initial species which was invested with the capability of multiplying into numerous species. And then He set in motion a natural process in the universe favourable to such multiplication. In this way, over a long period of time this primary species fulfilled its potential by changing into innumerable species. To put it another way, the theory of evolution is not a study of the existence of God, but simply of how God has displayed in the universe his power of creation. That is why Darwin himself has concluded his famous book The Origin of Species with these words:

There is grandeur in this view of life, that having been originally breathed by the Creator into a few forms or into one; and that, whilst this planet has gone cycling on according to the fixed law of gravity, from so simple a beginning endless forms most beautiful and most wonderful have been, and are being evolved (p. 408).

It is true that the new facts regarding the universe discovered in the twentieth century have revolutionised the world of logic. Now the difference between religious argument and scientific argument which had been erroneously conceived prior to the twentieth century, has been eliminated. Now in respect of argument, the case of science too has reached exactly the same point as religion.

Newton (1642-1727) made a special study of the solar system, discovering laws governing the revolution of planets around the sun. His study was, however, confined to astronomical bodies, which can be called the macro-world. It is possible in the macro world to weigh and measure things. As a result of the immediate impact of these discoveries, many began to think along the lines that reality was observable, and that proper and valid argument was one based on observation. It was under the influence of this concept that the philosophy generally known as positivism came into being.

However the discoveries made in the first quarter of the century shook the very foundation of their preliminary theories. These later discoveries revealed that beyond this world of appearance, a whole world was hidden, which does not come under observation. It is only indirectly possible to understand this hidden world and present arguments in its favour. That is, by observing the effects of something, we arrive at an understanding of its existence.

This discovery altered the whole picture. When the access of human knowledge was limited to the macro-cosmic world, man was a prey to this misapprehension. But when human knowledge penetrated the micro-world, the academic situation changed on its own.

Now it was revealed that the field of direct argument was extremely limited. New facts which came to the knowledge of man were so abstruse that indirect or inferential argument alone was applicable. For instance, The German scientist, Wilhelm Konrad Roentgen found in 1895 during an experiment that on a glass before him some effects were observable, despite the fact that there was no known link between his experiment and the glass. He concluded that there was an invisible radiation which was travelling at the speed of 186,000 miles per second. Due to the unknown nature of this radiation, Reontgen named it X-rays (*Encyclopaedia Britannica*, 19/1058).

The twentieth century has seen the discoveries of a number of things like X-rays, which do not come under direct human observation. However due, to their effects having come to the knowledge of man, it was not possible to deny their existence. As a result of modern research, not only were different departments of science revolutionized but the science of logic too saw basic changes.

Now inferential reasoning was also accepted as a valid method of reasoning, for, without this discoveries like X-rays, the scientific structure of the atom, the existence of Dark Matter, etc., could not have been explained.

After the extension of this method of reasoning in modern times, argument on religious faith has become as valid as reasoning on scientific concepts. Exactly the same inferential logic which was employed to prove the newly discovered concepts of science, was applicable to religious faiths to prove their veracity. Now differences in the criterion of logic have vanished.

Answer to a Question

At the end of his article Professor Badham writes:

> *And I have to acknowledge that the existence of so much evil and suffering in the world counts against any vision of an all-powerful and loving God (p. 7).*

Here I have to say that evil is a relative world. An evil is an evil so long as it cannot be explained. A doctor performs surgery on the patient's body, a judge sentences a criminal to be hanged. All this appears to be injustice, cruelty. But we do not call it so, simply because we have a proper explanation to give for the acts of the judge and the doctor. The same is true of the evil pointed out by the article writer.

The first point is that the evil existing in human society is not spread over the entire universe. Leaving aside the limited human world, the vast universe is perfect, par excellence. It is entirely free of any defect or evil.

Now the question arises as to why there is evil in the human world. To arrive at an understanding of this we shall have to understand the creation plan of the Creator. The creation plan of God provides the only criterion by which to judge the nature of the matter.

The creation plan of God as revealed to His Prophet is that this world is a testing ground, where man's virtue is placed on trial. It is in accordance with the records of this trial period that man's eternal fate will be decreed. It is for the purpose of this test that he has been granted freedom. In the absence of freedom, the question of life being a test would not arise.

The present evil is, in fact, a concomitant of this freedom. God desires to select those individuals who, in spite of being granted freedom, lead a disciplined and principled life. For individuals to prove their worth an atmosphere of freedom must be provided. Undoubtedly, due to such an atmosphere, some people will surely misuse this freedom and perpetrate injustice. But this is the inevitable price to be paid for such a creation plan to be brought to completion. No better creation plan can be envisaged for this world.

The present world appears meaningless when seen independently, that is, without joining the Hereafter with it. But when we take this world and the Hereafter together, the entire matter takes a new turn. Now this world becomes extremely meaningful and extremely valuable.

What is Islam

Every religion or system has a set of terminology which it is necessary to understand in order to have a proper appreciation of that particular religion or system. The religion of Islam too has its set of terminology. I would like here to present in brief certain basic terms.

1. Iman (Faith)

The literal meaning of *Iman* is to believe in or to have faith in something. That is, to accept Islam with conviction. This deep faith is attainable through realisation alone. Hence it would be proper to say that faith is a discovery and that there is no discovery greater than the discovery of God.

2. Islam (Surrender to God)

Islam means to submit or to surrender with a full realisation of God. Man abandons his ego, his freedom, and surrenders himself before God completely. In all matters of life he obeys God's commandments. He begins to lead a restrained life instead of a permissive one. This is what is called Islam.

3. Dhikr (Remembrance)

Dhikr means to remember—in Islamic terminology it means to remember God. When man discovers God, the Creator, the Almighty, Who will reward as well as punish for our good and bad deeds, it is inevitable that the thought of God comes to dominate one's mind. At all times and in all situations one remembers God. This remembrance is known as *dhikr*. When a person has reached this stage, this is a sure indication that he has found God with all His attributes.

4. Salat (Prayer)

Salat means prayer. It forms the most important part of Islamic worship. It is obligatory for a Muslim to offer prayer five times a day. Besides this, *Nafil* (voluntary prayer) may be said at other times. The spirit of *salah* is *khushu* which means submission. *Salat* is intended to inculcate a deep sense of submission in a believer, which is expressed externally by his physical bowing in the postures of *ruku* and *sajda*.

5. Sawm (Fasting)

The literal meaning of sawm is abstinence. *Sawm* is a form of worship which has to be observed annually, in the month of Ramadan. The outward form of *sawm* is abstinence from eating and drinking from morning till sunset. The inner state of *sawm* is renunciation of all things that God has forbidden, directly or indirectly. When a man fasts, observing all these aspects of fasing, spirituality is produced within him. He comes to experience closeness with God.

6. Zakat (alms-giving)

Zakat means purity. This means that a man purifies his earnings by giving away one part of them in the path of

God. In this way, *zakat* awakens the sense in man not to consider his earnings as his own possession, but a gift of God. *Zakat* is, in essence, a practical acknowledgement of God's bounties. And this admission is no doubt the greatest form of worship.

7. Hajj (Pilgrimage)

Hajj means pilgrimage. That is, visiting sacred places in Hijaz in the month of Zul Hijja in order to perform the annual worship of Hajj required of a believer once in a lifetime. Hajj is a symbol of Islamic unity. It is through Hajj that interaction takes place between Muslims on an international scale. Then it is also through Hajj that Muslims from all over the world are reminded of Abraham's sacrifice. On the pilgrimage they also witness the historical places associated with the Prophet of Islam. In this way they return with a long-lasting inspiration, which continues to activate them to adhere to the path of God throughout their lives.

8. Dawah (Invocation)

Dawah means to call, to invite. A Muslim who has received the message of God must do his utmost to communicate this message to other human beings. This dawah work in its nature is a prophetic task. The more one follows the way of the Prophet in the performance of this task, the greater the reward one will receive for it.

9. Jihad (Struggle)

The literal meaning of *jihad* is to strive or to struggle. In the present world, most of the time one has to work for Islam in adverse circumstances. In such circumstances, working for religion through struggle and sacrifice is called *jihad*. This jihad involves struggling with one's own self as well. Struggling to communicate the word of God to others is also *jihad*. In a similar way when any power commits aggression against Islam then, at that moment, rising in defence against that power too is jihad.

10. Sabr (Patience)

Sabr means patience, for example, restraining oneself from any adverse reaction when faced with an unpleasant situation. On all such occasions, one must be able to offer a positive response instead of a negative one. This is essential. For, in this present world, unpleasant events set in motion by others have to be faced time and again. If one is invariably provoked on such occasions and reacts negatively, the desired personality will not develop in one. All the teachings of religion require a positive psychology. Therefore, one who loses patience will be able neither to imbibe religious instruction nor to pass it on to others.

Behaviour of a Muslim in His Environment

(Selections from the Sayings of the Prophet Muhammad)

1. "You are helped and are provided for only because of the weak and poor ones among you." (*Bukhari*)

2. "I and the guardian of orphans (whether the orphan be of one's near or distant relation or of strangers) will be in one place in Paradise, like my two fingers", said the Prophet and his fingers were nearly touching each other at the time. (*Muslim*)

3. On one occasion a man complained to the Prophet of having a hard heart. The Prophet prescribed the following remedy "Touch an orphan's head and feed the poor". (*Ahmad*)

4. Someone said: 'O Prophet of God, teach me something'. "Abuse no one", replied the Prophet, 'and despise not anything good and speak to your fellow-men with open countenance". (*Tirmidhi*)

5. "God has no mercy for him who has no mercy for his fellows". (*Bukhari & Muslim*)

6. "A man came to the Prophet and said 'How many times should I forgive a servant?' The Prophet kept silent. The man repeated the question thrice.

"Forgive your servant seventy times everyday" said the Prophet. (*Abu Dawud*)

7. "He who does not behave kindly towards younger people and does not show due respect to older ones is not of us". (*Tirmidhi*)

8. Someone asked: 'What is Islam?' The Prophet said: "Purity of speech and hospitality." (*Musnad Ahmad*)

9. The Prophet said: 'On the Day of Judgment God will question: 'O Man, I was sick and you did not visit Me'. 'My Lord', the man will wonder, 'How could I visit You when You are the Lord of the universe?' God will remind: 'My so and so servant was sick and you did not visit him. Had you visited him, you would have found Me there, with him?' (*Muslim*).

10. "Visit the sick, feed the hungry, and help to relieve people's misery" (*Bukhari*).

11. 'Muslims who live in the midst of society and bear with patience the afflictions that come to them are better than those who shun society and cannot bear any wrong done to them'. (*Abu Dawud*)

12. "Every good deed is a charity, and it is a good deed that you meet your fellow-men with a cheerful countenance and you pour water from your bucket into the vessel of your fellow. Answering a questioner with mildness is charity. Removing that which is inconvenience to wayfarers, such as thorns and stones is charity". (*Tirmidhi*)

13. "The leader of a people is truly their servant." (*As-Suyuti*)

14. "Faith (iman) is to restrain oneself against all violence, let no believer commit any violence". (*Abu Dawud*)

15. "God has forbidden you disobedience of parents, miserliness, false claims, and the burying alive of female infants". (*Bukhari & Muslim*)

16. 'Give the worker his wages before his sweat dries'. (*Ibn Majah*)

17. "The seller is under obligation to disclose any defect in the article offered for sale". (*Bukhari*)

18. "No one should be subjected to chastisement by fire". (*Bukhari*)

19. "Honest difference of opinion among my people should be accounted a blessing." (*As-Suyuti*)

20. Someone asked the Prophet 'what fanaticism was?' and he replied: "That you help your people in wrongdoing". (*Abu Dawud*)

21. "That one will not enter Paradise whose neighbour is not secure against his mischief". (*Muslim*)

22. "He who believes in God and the Last Day must not put his neighbour to inconvenience." (*Bukhari & Muslim*)

23. "He is not a believer who eats to his fill while his neighbour goes without food." (*Ibn 'Abbas, Al-Baihiqi*)

24. The Prophet said: 'A person passing through a street carrying anything pointed or with a sharp edge should cover it up, so that nobody is exposed to the risk of injury due to his carelessness'. (*Muslim*)

25. "To remove anything from the street that causes inconvenience is charity". (*Bukhari*)

26. "God is Gentle and loves gentleness in all things". (*Bukhari & Muslim*)

27. "Gentleness adorns everything and its absence leaves everything defective". (*Muslim*)

28. 'Honour your children (esp. daughters) and make provisions for their proper up-bringing'. (*Ibn Majah*)

29. One who brings up three daughters, teaches them good manners and morals, arranges their marriages and treats them with fairness, deserves to be ushered

into Paradise. (*Abu Dawud*)

30. "Paradise lies at the feet of the mothers". (*As-Suyuti*)

31. On one occasion the Prophet observed: "Most unfortunate is the person whose parents are aged and who fails to win Paradise through taking good care of them". (*Bukhari*)

32. 'A man came seeking permission to participate in jihad (Holy War). The Prophet asked him: "Are your parents alive?" The man said: "Yes". He sent him away saying: "Then go back and find your jihad in serving them." (*Muslim*)

33. "He who wishes to enter Paradise through the best door must please his father and mother."

34. "The most perfect of believers in the matter of faith is he whose behaviour is best; and the best of you are those who behave best towards their wives". (*Tirmidhi*)

35. "You will not enter Paradise until you have faith, and you will not complete your faith until you love one another." (*Bukhari & Muslim*)

36. "He who eases the hardship of another, will have ease bestowed upon him by God in this world and the next... God goes on helping a servant so long as he goes on helping his fellow-man." (*Muslim*)

37. In his Farewell Address, the Prophet said: "You are all brothers and are all equal. None of you can claim any privilege or any superiority over any other. An Arab is not to be preferred to a non-Arab, nor is a non-Arab to be preferred to an Arab; nor is a white man to be preferred to a coloured one, or a coloured one to a white, except on the basis of righteousness." (*Musnad Ahmad*)

38. The Prophet, during his night prayer, used to say: "O God, I bear witness that all human beings are brothers". (*An-Nasa'i*)

39. Even with regard to servants, the Prophet said: "They are your brothers, and you must treat them as such. Provide them with the kind of clothes that you wear, and if you set them a hard task, join them in it to help them complete it". (*Abu Dawud*)

40. The Prophet observed: "None of you can be a believer unless he should desire for his fellow-man what he desires for himself." (*Bukhari*)

41. "He who defends the honour of his fellow-man, God will shield his face against the fire on the Day of Judgement". (*Tirmidhi*)

42. "God is not merciful to him who is not merciful to mankind."

43. "He who keeps away from his brother and fellow-man for a year is as if he had slain him." (*Abu Dawud*)

44. The Prophet was very insistent upon kindness towards animals. On one occasion he noticed a dove flying around agitatedly, and discovered that somebody had caught its young. He was very annoyed and asked the person to restore the young to the mother immediately. (*Abu Dawud*)

45. 'A woman was tormented on account of a cat which she had shut up till it died. On that account she entered the Fire.' (*Muslim*)

46. "Forgiveness was granted to an unchaste woman who, coming up on a dog panting and almost dead with thirst at the mouth of a well, took off her shoe, tied it with her head covering, and drew some water for it. On that account she was forgiven." (*Bukhari*)

47. "The Prophet forbade beating or branding an animal on its face." (*Muslim*)

48. "You will be rewarded by God for your acts of kindness towards all living creatures."

49. "There is no man who kills a sparrow, or any other

living creature (even it may be more despicable than a little sparrow) without its deserving it, but God will ask him about it". (*An-Nasa'i*)

50. "For a Muslim it is an act of charity to plant a tree or till a land where birds or people or animal come and eat of its fruits." (*al-Bazzar*)

51. "If a Muslim plants a tree or sows a field and men and beasts and birds eat from it, all of it is charity on his part". (*Muslim*)

52. "Even looking after plants and trees is an act of virtue." (*Ibn 'Asakir*)

53. "Whosoever gives a medicine, being not known in medicine, shall be held responsible for the consequence." (*Abu Dawud, Nasa'i*)

54. "Let no one ask another to give up his seat to him; but make room and sit at ease." (*Muslim*)

55. "When three persons are together, two of them must not whisper to each other without letting the third hear, because it would hurt him."

56. "He who takes a hand's breadth of land unjustly shall wear round his neck a garland composed of seven earths". (*Bukhari & Muslim*)

57. "Save yourselves from envy. For envy eats up virtue as fire eats up wood". (*Abu Dawud*)

58. "To earn through labour is the best way to earn, provided the work is done with sincerity". (*Ahmad*)

59. "When a man tells you something in confidence, you must not betray his trust". (*Abu Dawud*)

60. "Abdullah said that it was not proper to tell lies either in serious or in light vein. Neither was it proper to make promises to one's children and then not fulfill them". (*Bukhari & Muslim*)

Islam in the Modern World

The Prophet of Islam made a number of notable predictions which have been recorded in the books of hadith. One of the best known is that, in the final phase of human life on earth, the word of Islam will reach all human beings inhabiting this world. In other words, future times will see the intellectual ascendancy of Islam.

However, if the word of God is to be brought into every home, conditions must exist which will favour the success of such a mission. Without such conditions no such goal can be reached. Fortunately, recent studies show that as a result of revolutions occurring over the last several years, conditions now prevail which are more conducive than ever to the communication of the Islamic message. That process having been set in motion, individuals from different communities have begun embracing Islam in countries all over the world. Now, the need of the hour is for servants of God to arise and, by fully availing of new opportunities, play a decisive role in the last and most significant chapter of Islamic *da'wah*.

Da'wah is the real strength of Islam. It is through *da'wah* that Islam makes continuous progress. That is why, in every age, believers have seen fit to engage themselves in this task. Today, there are greater opportunities than hitherto to make Islamic *da'wah* a success. The communication of the message of God has certainly been going on in every age. But now modern circumstances have made it possible for this task to be performed with a greater degree of efficacy than ever before, and on a truly universal scale.

Today, opportunities to carry out *da'wah* work are legion. But I shall cite only a few examples to illustrate my point.

Proof of the Existence of God

Rationalists have habitually attempted to deny the existence of God by asking, "If God created the universe, who created God?" Now, as we are nearing the end of the 20th century, it has become possible to answer this question on a purely rational level. This new possibility arises out of the big bang theory, which has now gained general acceptance among cosmologists. With the big bang theory, we have necessarily to accept a first cause underlying the creation of the universe. That is, if there were no cause, the universe would not have existed. It has made it possible for us to tell the rationalists that all along they have been giving their attention to a wrong set of options. In their view, a choice had to be made between a universe with God and a universe without God, whereas the real choice was between a universe with God and no universe at all. Since we cannot opt for a non-existent universe, we are compelled to choose the universe with God.

Validity of Inferential Argument

To prove Islamic belief in the unseen world, our religious scholars have so far used inferential argument. That is, they suppose an unknown reality on the basis of a known reality. The rationalists' view of this argument was that its method was academically invalid, as it was based on the principle of indirect argument. They demanded to be given an argument of a direct nature. Only then would they accept it.

In this matter—as in material matters—the river of science has been flowing in favour of Islam. The above objection had apparently carried weight in the days when the study of science was macro-cosmic in scope. But as soon as scientific research began to delve into the micro-cosmic world, the balance tipped in favour of inferential argument. For it was revealed that the deeper realities of nature itself were those which did not come under the sphere of direct argument. For instance, the establishment of the existence of oxygen or X-rays is arrived at by indirect or inferential argument. Modern philosophers, such as Bertrand Russell, have demonstrated that inferential argument is as valid as indirect argument.

That is why, in science itself, inferential argument is held to be valid. Without it, scientific study could not be continued in the microcosmic world. In this way, a new chapter on unseen realities has been opened for the da'is.

I was once asked by a non-believer by what set of criteria I establish the existence of God. I replied that it was the self-same criteria on which he himself relied. He remained silent at this. For he knew full well that his own scientific concepts were proved by means of inferential argument. So when inferential argument is valid in non-religious fields, it will certainly be valid in the field of religion.

Historical Credibility of the Qur'an

In the present time, all manner of things, including religious scriptures, are being subjected to investigation in the spirit of free enquiry. A permanent discipline has been set up for this special study, called historical criticism, or higher criticism. Under this general heading, all great religious scriptures, including the Qur'an and the Bible, have been subjected to historical inquiry.

The results of these studies are entirely in favour of the Qur'an. They show that the Qur'an is the only religious scripture which is a historically accredited work. The rest of the books, having been shown to be dogmatic rather than historical, have lost their formal status as purveyors of eternal truth. Such research has provided a new and powerful argument in favour of Quranic veracity. That is to say, it is only the Qur'an which enjoys historical credibility. No other religious scripture is of similar merit.

This scientific discovery has brought Islam to the position of undisputed victory, for no other religion is capable of facing this academic test.

Scientific Verification

In ancient times, superstitious notions about every object of nature were given great credence, as is evident from the literature of those days. Now in modern times, when nature has been scientifically studied, many ancient concepts have been discredited. Books written in the pre-scientific age are now suspect—as belonging to the age of superstition. Even religious scriptures have not emerged unscathed, for the periodic interpolation of superstitious notions has reduced them to the level of non-sacred literature.

The Qur'an, on the contrary, being a preserved book, is exceptionally free from such apocryphal additions. There are numerous references to nature in the Qur'an, but none of these descriptions clashes with facts discovered by science. After making a study of several such statements enshrined in the Qur'an, Dr Maurice Bucaille concludes:

In view of the level of knowledge in Muhammad's day,
it is inconceivable that many of the statements in the
Qur'an which are connected with science could have
been the work of a man. It is, moreover, perfectly
legitimate, not only to regard the Qur'an as the
expression of a Revelation, but also to award it a very
special place, on account of the guarantee of authenticity
it provides and the presence in it of scientific statements
which, when studied today, appear as a challenge to
explanation in human terms.

Passing Modern Tests

New methods to determine the antiquity of ancient
objects have been evolved in modern times. One of these,
called carbon-14 dating or radio-carbon dating, was
developed just after the second world war. It gave the
stamp of credibility to many facts which had hitherto
remained unauthenticated. It was applied in one famous
instance to a mummified body, believed to be that of
Merneptah, a contemporary of Moses. The mummy,
discovered by Professor Loret in one of Egypt's pyramids,
did amazingly prove to date back to the time of Moses,
when subjected to this new technique of dating.

This same method of carbon dating was applied to the
Shroud of Turin, an old linen cloth bearing the imprint of
a human face—always thought to be the covering in which
Christ was wrapped after his crucifixion. According to this
belief, the cloth had to be two thousand years old. But
carbon dating revealed that it dated back no further than
the middle of the fourteenth century.

There are so many examples of this nature, that it is not
possible to deal with all of them. Suffice it to say that they
are symbolic of how modern sciences, on the one hand,
discredit ancient religions while, on the other hand, they
strengthen the credibility of Islam.

The Last Word

In modern times, great new opportunities have arisen for Islamic *da'wah*. This has made it possible for the first time to fulfill the prediction of the word of God being brought into each and every home. They point the way to Islam gaining the position of an ideological super power on a universal scale. But there is one necessary condition which is indispensable to the achievement of this goal. We shall have to adopt the same strategy in modern times as that adopted by the Prophet of Islam in the 19th year of his prophethood.

This historical strategy has come to be called the Hudaybiyya principle. This entails putting an end to the kind of controversies which create tension between the *da'i* and the *mad'u*. Without a normal atmosphere, free of friction, no *da'wah* action can be set in motion. Today the same controversial situation has come to exist between *da'i* and *mad'u* as was found between the Prophet and his hearers after the emigration. We must, therefore, follow the same Hudaybiyya principle as the Prophet did. This is the demand of the times, and in this lies the secret of all Muslim success.

PART II

The Spirit of Islam

Islam is the answer to the demands of nature. It is in fact a counterpart of human nature. This is why Islam has been called a religion of nature in the Qur'an and Hadith.

A man once came to the Prophet Muhammad and asked him what he should do in a certain matter. The Prophet replied, 'Consult your heart about it.' By the heart the Prophet meant common sense. That is, what one's commons sense tells one would likewise be the demand of Islam.

What does human nature desire more than anything? It desires, above all, peace and love. Every human being wants to live in peace and to receive love from the people around him. Peace and love are the religion of human nature as well as the demand of Islam. The Qur'an tells us, "..and God calls to the home of peace." (10:25)

One of the teachings of Islam is that when two or more people meet, they must greet one another with the words, *Assalamu-'Alaikum* (Peace be upon you). Similarly, Salat, or prayer, five times daily is the highest form of worship in Islam. At the close of each prayer all worshippers have to turn their faces to either side and utter the words *Assalamu-'Alaikum wa rahmatullah* (May peace and God's blessing be upon you). This is like a pledge given to people: 'O people you are safe from me. Your life, your property, your honour is secure with me.'

This sums up the spirit of true religion, the goal of which is spiritual uplift. It is the ultimate state of this spiritual uplift which is referred to in the Qur'an as the "soul at rest" (87:27).

Thus a true and perfect man, from the religious point of view, is one who has reached that level of spiritual development where nothing but peace prevails. When a person has attained that peaceful state, others will receive from him nothing but peace. He may be likened to a flower which can send out only its fragrance to man, it being impossible for it to emit a foul smell.

An incident relating to a saint very aptly illustrates the spirit of religion. The story goes that once a Muslim sufi was travelling along with his disciples. During the journey he encamped near a large grove of trees upon which doves used to perch.

During this halt one of the sufi's disciples aimed at one of the doves, killed it, cooked it and then ate it. Afterwards something strange happened. A flock of doves came to the tree under which the sufi was resting and began hovering over it and making a noise.

The Muslim sufi, communicating with the leader of the birds, asked what was the matter with them and why they were protesting. The leader replied, 'We have a complaint to make against you, that is, one of your disciples has killed one of us.' Then the Muslim sufi called the disciple in question and asked him about it. He said that he had not done anything wrong, as the birds were their foodstuff.

He was hungry, so he killed one for food. He thought that in so doing he had not done anything wrong. The sufi then conveyed this reply to the leader of the doves.

The latter replied: Perhaps you have failed to understand our point. Actually what we are complaining about is that all of you came here in the garb of sufis yet acted as hunters. Had you come here in hunter's garb, we would certainly have remained on the alert. When we saw you in the guise of sufis, we thought that we were safe with you and remained perched on the top of the tree without being properly vigilant.

This anecdote illustrates very well the reality of a true religious person or spiritual person for that matter. One who has reached the stage of spiritual uplift, and has found the true essence of religion no longer has the will or the capacity to do harm. He gives life not death, to others. He benefits others, doing no injury to anyone. In short, he lives among the people like flowers and not like thorns. He has nothing but love in his heart to bestow upon others.

Now I should like to say a few words about prayer and meditation in Islam. Let me begin with a question from the Qur'an:

> "When My servants question you about Me, tell them that I am near. I answer the prayer of the suppliant when he calls to Me; therefore, let them answer My call and put their trust in Me, that they may be rightly guided" (2:186).

This verse of the Qur'an tells us that in Islam there is no need for any intermediary to establish contact between God and man. At any time and place man can contact God directly. The only condition is that man should turn to God with sincere devotion.

Islam believes in a personal God. God is an alive being, fully aware of His servants. He hears and sees. That being so, man must call God in all personal matters. Whenever he calls God with a sincere heart, he will find Him close by.

Meditation in Islam aims at bringing man closer to God. When man worships God, when he remembers Him, when his heart is turned towards Him in full concentration, when he makes a request or a plea, then he establishes a rapport with his Maker. In the words of the Hadith, at that particular moment he comes to whisper with his Lord. He has the tangible feeling that he is pouring his heart out to God and that God in turn is answering his call.

When this communion is established between God and man, man can feel himself becoming imbued with a special kind of peace. His eyes are moist with tears. He starts receiving inspiration from God. It is in moments such as these that man can rest assured of his prayers being granted by God.

According to a *hadith* the Prophet Muhammad said the highest form of worship is to pray as if you were seeing God. We learn from this *hadith* the true sign of a superior form of worship. The true sign is for man to sense the presence of God during worship, and feel that he has come close to God. That is when he can experience the refreshing, cooling effect of God's love and blessings for man. It is this feeling of closeness to God which is the highest form of spiritual experience.

Spiritual Unity

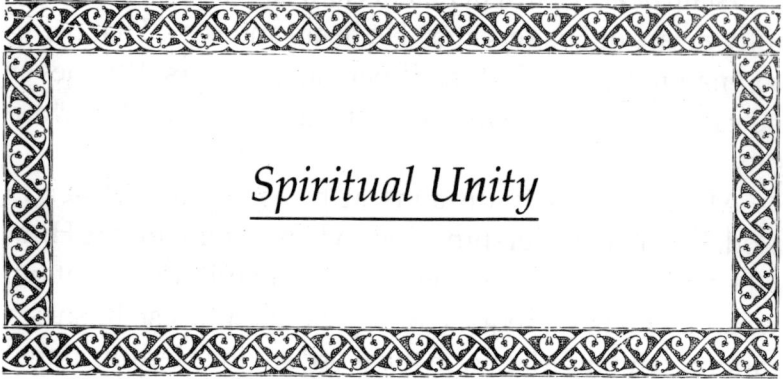

It is generally said that in present times, the world has assumed the form of a global village. But this is only half the truth. Modern technology and communications have, of course, greatly reduced distances across the world. But the closeness thus produced is of a purely physical nature. Modern technology may have bridged certain gaps, bringing the external world closer together, but the task of bringing unity into the internal world has yet to be accomplished.

What is spiritual unity? Let us take a very simple example. When you live in a crowded settlement, the walls all around give you a sense of limitation. You experience the friction of living in close contact with others and you suffer from mental tension. Later, when you emerge from that dense human settlement into open, natural surroundings you immediately feel that your tension has evaporated and you have once again become serene. You feel that you have joined a limitless universality. The feeling of separateness is replaced by an all-pervasive feeling of unity. You immediately become part of a world where there are no boundaries. A sense of universality prevails.

We have all had this experience at one time or another. It shows us what spiritual unity is. It is, in fact, the raising of one's existence to a higher plane. The moment you achieve this, you feel you are emerging from a limited world to become a citizen of an unlimited world. Disunity now disappears, giving way to unity all around.

Although, physically, all human beings appear to be different, spiritually they are one. It is as if spiritual unity between human beings already exists, it does not have to be externally imposed. We have only to make people aware of its existence. Once the outer, artificial veils are removed, what remains will be pure spirituality.

In reality, the various sets of circumstances that confront man in this world lead to drawing of different veils over man's natural propensities. For instance, the veil of material greed produces self-centredness; the veil of jealousy causes him to see himself as being separate from others; the veil of prejudice causes him to discriminate between human beings, and so on.

These veils, in fact, tend to block man's natural urge towards spiritual unity. What is required is to remove these artificial veils in order that the true, inner reality be brought into focus.

The aim of all religions, basically, is to encourage this spiritual unity within man and between man and man. No religion is at variance with another so far as this goal is concerned. The language in which this is set forth may vary from one religion to another, but, without doubt, the main concern of all religions is to produce spiritual unity within and between all human beings. Without spiritual unity, there is little hope of creating peace and harmony throughout the world. And where there is no peace and harmony, the dream of human progress will for ever remain elusive.

Now, what is Islam's contribution to spiritual unity? The subject is too vast for more than just a few basic points to be briefly touched on.

The Unity of God

The most important factor in Islam's contribution is its concept of monotheism—of there being only one God (2:163). According to Islam, God, or the ultimate reality of this universe is only one—called Allah in Islam. It is implicit in the concept of the oneness of Godhead that differences and multiplicity would appear to exist in reality, yet there is an underlying unity.

In this way the concept of divine unity engenders spiritual unity. All human beings are one, because they are the servants of one God. All human beings are God's family. God is indeed the greatest reality of the universe. And when it is acknowledged that there is only one greatest reality, it is but natural that all other creation should acquire the character of unity.

The Unity of Nature

The Qur'an states that "There is no changing in God's creation." (30:30) According to the Prophet of Islam 'every child is born with an upright nature.' (Al-Bukhari) We learn from this that unity is found among all human beings at the level of nature and creation. Nature forms the common constituent in the creation of human beings, just as the atom forms the common constituent in all the varied objects of nature in the physical world. That is to say that the same unity which exists in the external world at the physical level, has existed among human beings at the spiritual level from the outset.

But man tends at times to be oblivious of his own nature. This is no less true in the sphere of unity. Today people are unaware of their spiritual potential. In such a situation, the easiest way to bring about spiritual unity is to make men aware of that potential. The moment they became aware of it, spiritual unity will come into existence of its own accord.

The Unity of Mankind

The Qur'an says, "O Men, have fear of your Lord, who created you from a single soul. From that soul He created its mate, and through them, He scattered the earth with countless men and women." (4:1)

This shows that men and women have been created from the same substance. Their being physically one, of necessity, demands their spiritual oneness.

Making a similar point, the Prophet Muhammad said that all human beings are brothers (Abu Dawud). This gives rise to the concept of a common brotherhood, and without doubt, it is this sense of brotherhood which generates the strongest feeling of oneness and togetherness among different people.

That is to say that when all human beings in this world are virtually blood brothers, they must, as this concept necessarily demands, live as brothers in spirit too. Any other way of living is a deviation from the reality.

I should like to refer here to an incident which illustrates this point. In 1893, Swami Vivckananda went to Chicago to participate in the Parliament of Religions. As the *Encyclopaedia Britannica* puts it, his was a 'sensational appearance.' (15/623) On that occasion all the speakers at the conference followed the common practice of addressing the audience as "Ladies and gentlemen." But when Swami Vivekananda took the stage, he addressed his hearers as "Sisters and brothers of America." No sooner were the words out of his mouth than the hall resounded with a long burst of applause. Of all the delegates at the conference, Swamiji received the greatest ovation.

The reason for this was that the form of address, "Ladies and gentlemen" produces a sense of alienation and strangeness, whereas the phrase "Sisters and Brothers" introduces a note of closeness and familiarity. By using this phrase, Swami Vivekananda touched a cord in the hearts of those of different creeds and colours. Their natural feeling of unity was awakened, and then what ensued fulfilled the best of expectations. All of a sudden, the gaps between them were bridged. They all began to feel themselves what they really were, and for that moment, physical divisions disappeared and were replaced by a rare spiritual unity.

The Spiritual Goal of Islam

That is the spiritual goal of Islam? That is, what is that spiritual target which Islam sets before man? The answer in the words of the Qur'an is: 'A soul at rest' (89:27). Thus the spiritual goal of Islam is to attain this state of peace in the soul.

According to the Qur'an this is the ultimate stage in a man's spiritual development. When he reaches this stage of progress, he qualifies himself to be ushered into Paradise, the perfect and eternal world of the Hereafter. The Qur'an addresses such souls in these words: 'O serene soul! Return to your Lord joyful, and pleasing in His sight. Join My servants and enter My paradise' (89:27-30).

In this world man has to lead his life in circumstances in which he experiences various kinds of situations: there are times of gain, times of loss; times of happiness and times of grief. Sometimes he receives good treatment at the hands of others, at other times his fate is quite otherwise.

The ideal human being of the Qur'an is one who undergoes all these experiences without losing his integrity. Under no circumstances is his inner peace disturbed.

However, untoward the occasion, he can maintain his natural balance. Success does not make him proud. Power does not make him haughty. No bad treatment by others drives him to seek vengeance in anger. At all events, he remains serene. It is such a man who is called 'a peaceful soul' in the Qur'an. And it is this man who, according to the Qur'an, has achieved the highest spiritual state.

The realization of God joins man to his Maker. Such communion with the divine brings about a state of spiritual elevation. Having been thus raised to a higher plane of existence, man becomes of a 'sublime character,' (68:4) as it is expressed in the Qur'an.

This can be illustrated by an example from the natural world: The process of conversion of a substance from the solid to the gaseous state, is called boiling. The boiling point of a liquid varies according to atmospheric pressure. At sea level, water boils at 100 degrees centigrade. At a higher altitude, as on a mountain, the atmospheric pressure is less, so the boiling point is lower. This shows that it is the altitude that makes the difference.

The law of nature governing this world accounts for the difference made by altitude. Islam's aim is to foster human beings whose altitude has changed. The superior qualities desired in him will come later, on their own.

Just as the Prophet of Islam was God's messenger, so also was he a perfect example of the peaceful soul. By studying his life, one can learn the nature of God's ideal man, that is, a peaceful soul. In the Qur'an the Prophet Muhammad is described as an example of "sublime character" (68:4).

When is it that a man's spiritual progress brings him to the state of peace? The best way to describe the soul being at complete rest is to give certain examples from the life of the Prophet of Islam.

The Prophet's name was Muhammad, meaning the praised one or the praiseworthy. But when the Meccans became his most dire opponents, they themselves coined a name for the Prophet, 'Muzammam,' on the pattern of 'Muhammad,' Muzammam meaning condemned. They used to heap abuses on him calling him by this epithet of Muzammam. But the Prophet was never enraged at this distorted version of his name. All he said in return was: "Aren't you surprised that God has turned away the abuses of the Quraysh from me. They abuse a person by the name of Muzammam. Whereas I am Muhammad (Ibn Hisham, 1/379).

This meant that abuses were being heaped on a person whose name was Muzammam. Since the Prophet's name was Muhammad, not Muzammam, their abuses did not apply to him. Such a reaction can come only from a person whose intellectual level is very high; who can rise above praise and criticism.

One day the Prophet was sitting with his companions in Madinah when a funeral procession passed by. The Prophet stood up. His Companions pointed out that it was the funeral of a Jew, that is, a non-Muslim. The Prophet replied: 'Was he not a human being?' (Fathul Bari, 3/214).

This incident shows that the Prophet was looking at the matter by separating two different aspects of the Jew, that is, his being non-Muslim, and his being a human being. At that moment he overlooked his non-Muslim identity and saw him simply as a human being.

It is only a man who, in the words of the Qur'an has acquired a sublime character who can show such respect for every human being. It is only one whose spiritual progress has elevated his mental level who can do honour to one of another creed.

On another occasion the Prophet of Islam was in the Masjid al-Nabavi in Medina, the second most sacred mosque in Islam, when a Bedouin, that is, a desert Arab, entered the mosque and urinated inside it. It was obviously a very provocative matter. But the Prophet was not at all provoked. After the nomad had urinated, the Prophet simply asked his companions to bring a bucket of water and wash the place clean (*Fathul Bari,* 1/386).

This is a clear example of the kind of behaviour one may expect of a man with a peaceful soul. The Prophet's keeping cool at such obvious provocation was possible only because he had attained the highest state of spirituality. He had risen above all negative feelings.

These examples make it clear what a peaceful soul is. The peaceful soul is one which being on a higher spiritual plane, can live in tranquillity, regardless of the circumstances. It subsists within its own self. No external event can disturb its inner peace.

Nowadays people often tend to look at the history of kings in order to understand Islam. But this is not the proper way to study it. One needs only to study the careers of today's political leaders to be able to understand the nature of the Muslim kings of bygone days. Today's political leaders are, in reality, exploiters. In a similar way most of the Muslim kings of the later phase of Islam were also exploiters. To achieve their political ends, they exploited the name of Islam. As such, these Muslim kings were in no way the true representatives of Islam.

To me, those known as sufis or Muslim mystics were far better representatives of the spirit of Islam. The Muslim sufis embraced such values of Islam as love, peace, and kindness, and made an effort to spread these virtues all over the world. And that is the true spirit of Islam.

At this point, I would like to relate certain incidents relating to Muslim sufis, which illustrate their mission and which throw light on the real spirit of Islam.

Sheikh Nizamuddin Aulia was a great Muslim Sufi of the 13th century. The story goes that once a disciple of the Sheikh visited him. He offered him a gift of a pair of scissors, a product of his home town. When the Sheikh saw this gift, he remarked politely:

> 'What am I to do with this gift? It would have been better had you brought me a needle and thread. Scissors cut things apart, while a needle and thread join things together. You know my job is to unite people, and not to separate them.'

Maulana Ashraf Ali Thanawi, a famous sufi of India, one day arose to perform his ablutions. Having been brought a jug of water by his disciple, he sat down at one place to begin his ablutions, but then he got up again and went to another place. From there too he got up. Only when he had gone to a third place did he finally perform his ablutions.

The disciple found this very strange. With proper reverence he observed, 'Sir, you have done something new. Twice you sat at different places and then got up and finally you performed your ablutions at a third place.' Maulana Thanawi answered that at the first two places he had found ants creeping about on the ground. He thought that if he dropped water on them, they would be in trouble. Finally he had gone to a third place where there were no ants, and only then did he perform his ablutions.

This shows that when we should not harm even tiny creatures such as ants and earthworms, the harming of human beings is out of question. We ought to live in this world doing no harm and giving no pain. That is in the true spirit of Islam.

These anecdotes very aptly illustrate the reality of a true mystic or spiritual person. One who has reached an advanced stage of spiritual uplift, having found the true essence of religion, no longer has the will or the capacity to do harm. He gives others life, not death. He benefits others, doing injury to no one. In short, he lives among the people like the rose and not the thorn. He has nothing but love in his heart to bestow upon others.

Conclusion

To sum it up, according to Islam, the highest spiritual goal for man is his spiritual uplift when he has attained the high state called 'peaceful soul' in the Qur'an. This may also be termed as complex-free soul which can withstand all kinds of negativity.

Thus a developed or complex-free soul is one which, having reached a high level of thinking, has risen from all kinds of negativity and has attained a positive identity in the full sense of the word.

The importance of the peaceful soul, according to Islam, is its being deserving of salvation and thus eligible to enter the purest and finest realm of paradise.

The way to reach the stage of the peaceful soul depends upon man's relation to God. The more man turns his attention to God, the more he will receive inspiration from Him. With the help of divine inspiration, he will be able to pass through the various stages of spiritual uplift until he ultimately reaches that pinnacle of sublimity so desired by the Almighty.

This paper was presented by Maulana Wahiduddin Khan at a conference held by the Institute of Gandhian Studies, Wardha, on September 22, 1995.

Prayer in Islam

Du'a (prayer) literally means to call. In Islamic terminology du'a means calling God, whether for worldly assistance or for salvation in the Hereafter.

Prayer has great significance in Islam. According to one of the *hadith*, the Prophet Muhammad said, 'It is prayer (du'a) which is worship,' and 'Prayer is the essence of *'ibadah.*'[1] The reason prayer has such importance is that it is the ultimate expression of God's greatness and power and of man's helplessness. That is why a sincere prayer is the most precious of all deeds in the eyes of God.

Prayer does not mean learning certain words by rote and then constantly repeating them. Although many prayers have been recorded in the books of Hadith, they are meant only to give us the substance of prayer, not its wording.

Prayer, in fact, is the expression of a distressed state of the heart. Such a state of the heart cannot be bound within

---

[1] A technical term in theology meaning act of worship or ritual from the word 'abada "to serve" and 'abd "slave."

certain set words of prayer. True prayer comes from the lips of a person when, on the one-hand, he learns the full meaning of being a servant of God and, on the other, he discovers God in all His perfection. The words which come to his lips spontaneously with this two-sided realization are called prayer in the Islamic Shari'ah.

The concept of prayer in Islam and how to offer a true prayer is described in great detail in the Qur'an and Hadith. Here I should like to present some Quranic references.

1. Firstly prayer should be made to one God alone. The Qur'an says: 'Do not pray to anyone other than God, which can neither help nor harm you' (10:106). The Prophet Muhammad said: 'Whenever for anything you have to ask, it from God.' This is quite consistent with Islamic belief in monotheism. When Islam teaches mankind to believe in one God, with all power vested in Him alone, then praying to someone other than God can never be in accordance with Islam. That is why the Qur'an has this to say: 'His is the true prayer.' (13:14)

2. Prayer should always be marked by sincerity. The Qur'an says: 'Call to God, with sincere devotion to Him.' (40:14) When we conceive of God as being able to see one's heart, that prayer alone is of value wherein man's heart is fully in accord with his lips. A prayer which comes from one's lips alone is inconsistent with God's Majesty. Such a prayer certainly deserves to be rejected by God.

3. Prayer is the call of the helpless to the Almighty. It is therefore essential that it should be imbued with appropriate feelings. The Qur'an says: 'The faithful call on Us with piety, fear and submission.' (21:90) The Qur'an further says: 'Call on your Lord with humility and in private.' (7:55) When the suppliant has a correct perception

of God, his prayer will of necessity be imbued with such feelings.

4. God disapproves of man 'praying for evil as fervently as He prays for good.' (17:11) Praying for good is in accordance with man's humble position. True belief in God inculcates in man a temperament of sympathy and of kindness. One so inclined will always pray for good, he will never pray for evil.

5. According to a *hadith* the Prophet Muhammad said that God is best pleased when man prays to Him for peace (*Al-Tirmizi*). God likes peace. The Prophet frequently used to say this prayer: "O God! You are peace, and peace is from You. O God, help us to live with peace and reside in the home of peace, O Lord of Majesty and Glory." This invocation sums up the spirit of prayer.

6. Addressing the Prophet, God says in the Qur'an: 'When My servants question you about Me, tell them that I am near. I answer the prayer of the suppliant when he calls to Me.' (2:186) In Islam there is no intermediary between God and man. God is so near to man that He can always be called upon at any moment. According to Islam, the believers need neither an intermediary, nor any particular time or place to ask for anything from Him. Whenever he feels the need, and in whatever condition he may be, he can always establish contact with God.

I should like to sum this up by quoting a part of a sermon by Jesus Christ, relating to prayer. These words of Jesus Christ, to which Islam also subscribes, are the very essence of prayer:

> Ask, and you will receive; seek, and you will find;
> knock, and the door will be opened to you. For everyone
> who asks will receive, and anyone who seeks will find,
> and the door will be opened to him who knocks. Would

any of you who are fathers give your son a stone when he asks for bread? Or would you give him a snake when he asks for a fish? Bad as you are, you know how to give good things to your children. How much more, then, will your Father in heaven give good things to those who ask him! (Matthew 7:7-11).

Social Aspect of Islamic Mysticism

Eysticism is generally called *tasawwuf* in India and *irfan* (realization) in Iran. To me *irfan* is the most appropriate word for mysticism, in actual fact, it is another name for the realization of inner reality.

The word mysticism has been variously defined in academic works. By way of a simple definition, it means to penetrate one's inner soul and to enable it, by developing it, to establish contact with God, the Greater Soul.

This process purifies the human personality, and the soul comes to realize itself. The latent natural potential of the soul is ultimately awakened; in the words of the Quran, it becomes the serene (89:27) or pure soul (87:14).

It is but natural that the personality developed by the mystic (or the *Aarif*) in this way does not remain enclosed within a boundary. His inner state also having its external manifestation, his personality finds expression in his social relations.

One who has realized himself will, at the same time, place a higher spiritual value on other human beings too. One whose heart is filled with God's love, will necessarily be filled with the love of human beings—the creatures of

God. One who respects the Higher Reality will surely respect other human beings. It is this aspect of mysticism which I have called its social aspect.

A Persian mystic poet has expressed the mystic code of behaviour in these most beautiful words:

"The stories of kings like Alexander and Dara hold no interest for us. Ask us only about love and faithfulness."

Another mystic poet has this to say:

"The comforts of both the worlds are hidden in these two things: Being kind to friends and according better treatment to foes."

When a sufi or mystic is engrossed in the love of God, he rises above the mundane world and discovers the higher realities. He becomes such a human being as has no ill-feelings for anyone. In fact, he cannot afford hatred, as hatred would nullify his very spirituality. He cannot divest himself of feelings of love as this would amount to divesting himself of all delicate feelings.

Islam is the answer to the demands of nature. It is in fact a counterpart of human nature. This is why Islam has been called a religion of nature in the Qur'an and Hadith.

A man once came to the Prophet Muhammad and asked him what he should do in a certain matter. The Prophet replied, 'Consult your conscience (heart) about it.' By the conscience the Prophet meant his finer feelings. That is, what one's conscience tells one would likewise be what Islam would demand of one as a matter of common sense.

What does human nature desire more than anything? It desires, above all, peace and love. Every human being wants to live in peace and to receive love from the people around him. Peace and love are the religion of human nature as well as what Islam demands of us. The Qur'an tells us, "...and God calls you to the home of peace" (10:25).

One of the teachings of Islam is that when two or more people meet, they must greet one another with the words, *Assalamu-'Alaikum* (Peace be upon you). Similarly, *Salat*, or prayer, said five times daily is the highest form of worship in Islam. At the close of each prayer all worshippers have to turn their faces to either side and utter the words *Assalamu-'Alaikum wa rahmatullah* (May peace and God's blessing be upon you). This is like a pledge given to people: 'O people, you are safe from me. Your life, your property, your honour is secure with me.'

This sums up the spirit of true religion, the goal of which is spiritual uplift. It is the ultimate state of this spiritual uplift which is referred to in the Qur'an as the "serene soul" (89:27).

Thus a true and perfect man, from the Islamic point of view, is one who has reached that level of spiritual development where peace and peace alone prevails. When a person has attained that peaceful state, others will receive from him nothing less than peace. He may be likened to a flower which can send out only its fragrance to man, it being impossible for it to emit an unpleasant smell.

Islamic mysticism elevates people. It makes them think spiritually rather than materially. This spiritual elevation generates tolerance. People feel good about forgiving others. They eschew taking revenge. They return love for hatred. This kind of temperament is bound to establish peace and mutual respect. In this way, Islamic mysticism, in the practical sense, is the key to a good and peaceful society.

Now I should like to say a few words about prayer and meditation. Let me begin with a quotation from the Qur'an:

"When My servants question you about Me, tell them that I am near. I answer the prayer of the suppliant when he calls to Me; therefore, let them answer My call and put their trust in Me, that they may be rightly guided (2:186).

This verse of the Qur'an tells us that, in Islam, there is no need for any intermediary to establish contact between God and man. At any time and place man can contact God directly. The only condition is that man should turn to God with sincere devotion.

Islam believes in a personal God. God is an alive being, fully aware of His servants. He hears and sees. That being so, man must call upon God in all personal matters. Whenever he calls upon God with a sincere heart, he will find Him close by.

Meditation in Islam aims at bringing man closer to God. When man worships God, when he remembers Him, when his heart is turned towards Him with full concentration, when he makes a request or a plea, then he establishes a rapport with his Maker. In the words of the Hadith, at that particular moment he comes to whisper with his Lord. He has the tangible feeling that he is pouring his heart out to God and that God in turn is answering his call.

When this communion is established between God and man, man can feel himself becoming imbued with a special kind of peace. His eyes are moist with tears. He starts receiving inspiration from God. It is in moments such as these that man can rest assured of his prayers being granted by God.

According to a *hadith* the Prophet Muhammad said the highest form of worship is to pray as if you were seeing God. We learn from this *hadith* the true sign of a superior form of worship. The true sign is for man to sense the presence of God during worship, and feel that he has come close to God. That is when he can experience the refreshing, cooling effect of God's love and blessings for man. It is this feeling of closeness to God which is the highest form of spiritual experience.

PART III

The Importance of Studying the Life of the Prophet Muhammad and its Application to Our Lives

Dr. Michael H. Hart, in his now famous book, called *The Hundred—A Ranking of the Most Influential Persons in History*, has held the Prophet Muhammad, upon whom be peace, to be the most supremely successful man in history. But if the Prophet occupies this top-ranking position, it is not as a hero' although he had many heroic qualities—but as a guide to humanity. Throughout his life, not only was he a supremely successful person himself, but he also stood out as a superb model for others to imitate. It is this aspect of his seerah, or biography, which is outlined in this paper.

Beginning with the Possible

At the time that the Prophet came to the world, Arabia was racked by a multiplicity of problems. The Roman and Sassanid empires had made political inroads into Arabia; society was beset by evils such as usury, adultery, excessive drinking and senseless bloodshed; there still stood in the Kabah no less than 360 idols.

It is significant that the first commandment in the Qur'an was revealed to the Prophet was not about purifying the Kabah of idols, or waging war on the Persians and

Byzantines, or punishing criminals and wrongdoers according to the Shariah. On the contrary, the first commandment was concerned with reading, that is, with education. This is a clear indication that the proper starting point for Islamic activism must remain within the realm of the possible. At the time of the Prophet's advent, the prevailing circumstances in Arabia did demand the purification of the mosque, political stability and the imposition of Shariah law, yet, in spite of all the urgency for and desirability of such steps, they were in practice, impossible to implement. On the other hand, a beginning made on the basis of dawah, coupled with education, was conceivably within reach. The Prophet, divinely inspired as he was, made a point, therefore, of shunning the impossible in favour of the possible, whenever he engaged himself in Islamic activism. There is a saying in English which goes: "Politics is the art of the possible". The way of the Prophet was also to begin from the possible.

Ease in Difficulty

When Prophet of Islam and his early companions began communicating the message of monotheism in Mecca, it seemed that Meccan soil would yield up little to Islam except problems and difficulties. At that point in time a verse of the Qur'an was revealed which offered consolation and guidance. It said, "Every hardship is followed by ease. Every hardship is followed by ease." (94:5) It was because the Prophet was inspired by this belief that he was able to define and pursue a course of action which would ensure success. This was a very important aspect of the Prophet's approach to any difficult situation. The fact of his success proves, moreover, that God never intended this world to be one of endless difficulties—with never a solution in sight. It was the will of the Almighty that all difficulties should be resolvable; alongside apparent disadvantages which were also a part of the divine scheme. It was just a quesion of human beings having the confidence to acknowledge this fact, and then to seek out appropriate solutions.

One instance of ease counterbalancing difficulty was the existence of believers alongside unbelievers, two notable examples being Umar and Abu Jahal, who both lived in Mecca in the early days. Then even if it was impossible at that time to cleanse Kabah of idols, it was still quite possible to convince people that the worship of these false gods was an evil. Seen in this light, the difficulties faced by the believers in the first phase of Islam were, in fact, challenges which awakened Muslim potential, ultimately transforming each Muslim —in the word of Margolith— into a hero.

This aspect of recorded life of the Prophet shows that whenever believers find themselves in a quandary they should feel convinced from the very outset that, side by side with their problems, opportunities for their resolution do exist. Instead of lamenting over difficulties as if they were insuperable they must set about grasping such opportunities as will set them on the path to progress.

Emigration: Changing the Place of Action

In the early days of the Prophet's mission in Mecca his activities aroused such antagonism that his opponents made the ruthless decision to eliminate him. At that juncture, the Prophet chose to avoid confrontation by quietly leaving Mecca for Madina. It is this journey which is known as the hijrah, or emigration.

The Prophet's emigration, or self-exile, was a matter of strategy rather than an unwilling departure from his home town. He made this move advisedly in order to change the place of action. When he found Mecca an unfavourable place for his activities, he chose Madina as the new centre from which to continue his mission.

From this the principle was established that if believers found their environment so hostile that any continuance of their activities could lead to martyrdom at the hands of their enemies, it was quite proper for them to avoid direct confrontation and to move to a more suitable place for missionary action. Such a manoeuvre guaranteed keeping their mission alive, and also held out the possibility of eventually bringing Mecca within the fold.

Having Trust in Human Nature

The Prophet of Islam and his companions were repeatedly subjected to acts of antagonism by the unbelievers. They had to listen to provocative language, they had all kinds of obstacles placed in their path and they were even pelted with stones. At that time the Qur'an enjoined upon them the return of good for evil. And then, as the Qur'an added encouragingly, 'you will see your direst enemy has become your dearest friend'. (41:34)

From this injunction the important truth may be infered that no matter how hostile a man may appear, he has, nevertheless, a nature which is God-given, and truth-loving. It is as if beneath the outer surface of his antagonism there lies a hidden friend. If one is a dayee, that is, a genuine exponent of truth, one may feel reassured at all times that one's dawah, or mission, will strike a chord in the heart of one's listener.

The surest way to uncover this favourable aspect of an ill-disposed person is to return good behaviour for bad behaviour. Our own continuing good behaviour will rub off the veneer of hostility so that the friendly inner core may stand revealed. It is a matter of historical record that in the first phase of Islam, tens of thousands of people entered its fold because they were encouraged to do so by da'is acting on this principle. For example, there was an idolater who, on finding the Prophet alone, drew his sword to kill him, but he was so overawed by the Prophet's unflinching courage in the face of his threat, that the sword dropped from his hand. Then it was the Prophet's turn to retaliate. But instead of retaliating, the Prophet forgave him. His would- be assailant was so highly impressed by his extraordinary character, that he immediately accepted Islam.

Making the Best of One's Enemies

After the Battle of Badr, about 70 of the enemy were taken prisioner. All of them belonged to Mecca and all of them were educated. The Prophet announced that any of these war criminals who were willing to teach ten children of Madina how to read and write would be freed. Their services would be taken in lieve of ransom money. This was the first school in the history of Islam in which all of the students were Muslims, and all of the teachers were from the enemy ranks.

THE POWER OF PEACE

An important lesson to be derived from the Prophet's life is that the power of peace is stronger than the power of violence. The power the Prophet made use of more than any other in his whole life was that of peace. For instance, when Mecca was conquered, all his direst opponents who had tortured him, expelled him from his home town, launched military onslaughts against him, and inflicted all sorts of harm on him and his companions, were now brought before him. These people were undeniably war criminals and as such, could expect to be put to death by the victor, that being the common practice at that time. Yet the Prophet did not utter so much as a word of blame. He simply said, "Go, you are all free."

This sublime gesture to men who stood on the thereshold

of the grave, demonstrated the superiority of peace over violence. The result of the Prophet' elevated moral behavior was their immediate acceptance of Islam.

The Third Option

In the last days of the Prophet, a battle called Ghazwa Mu'tah took place between Muslims and Romans in the region, now known as Jordan. In a matter of days, twelve of the companions were martyred. At that point, Khalid Ibn Walid, who had just been appointed commander of the Muslim army, was advised that the Romans numbered two hundred thousand, while the Muslims numbered a mere three thousand. Considering this huge difference in numbers an insurmountable obstacle to Muslim victory, he decided to withdraw his forces from the battlefield.

When he and his men reached Madina, some of the Madinan Muslims gave them a humiliating reception by calling out to them a 'O deserters!' The Prophet thereupon said, "They are not deserters but—Insha Allah—action takers."

There was a kind of flawed dichotomy in the thinking of those Medinan Muslims. In their view, there were but two options: one was to fight the enemy courageously, and the other was to beat an ignominious retreat. Since they thought that the Muslim army should have stayed with the first option, even if it meant that each and every one of them was martyred in the process.

On this occasion, the Prophet of Islam pointed to the existence of a third option. And that was to remove themselves from the field of action to a place where, undisturbed by war, they could build up their strength and prepare intensively for a more effective campaign at a later date. The return of Khalid ibn Walid from Muta was not as such, a retreat, but rather adherence to this third option. History tells us, in fact, that the Muslims after 3 years of such preparation, went back under the command of Usamah ibn Zayd to the Roman borders and where they won a resounding victory.

A change in the Field of Action

When the Prophet Muhammad migrated from Mecca to Medina, the Meccan leaders, still not content, launched an all-out offensive against him. Several military engagements ensued without their being a decisive victory in sight. Ultimately, the Prophet entered into a pact with the Meccans at Hudaybiyyah. This, in effect, was a 10 year peace treaty which permitted the Prophet to change the arena of action and to look forward to a long and undisturbed period of missionary activity. Till then, the meeting ground between Muslims and non-Muslims had been on the battlefield. Now the area of conflict became that of ideological debate. Very soon after this agreement was signed, the one-time enemies began interacting with each other on a large scale. During this period of interaction, the ideological superiority of the Muslims so asserted itself that large numbers of their former enemies began to enter the fold of Islam. In this way, the number of Muslims continuously increased, with a corresponding decrease in the numbers of non-Muslims. Ultimately the Muslims came to occupy a dominating position—without doing battle—solely on the strength of their greater numbers.

The success, in this instance, of the Prophet's methods lends conviction to the view that if the believers are repeatedly thwarted in bringing their missionary struggle to fruition, it is only proper that their efforts should be re-deployed in some other field of action where more positive results may be expected.

The Principle of Gradualism

According to a tradition related by Aishah, and recorded

in the writings of Bukhari, when Qur'anic revelations began, the first verses to be communicated were those which mentioned hell and heaven. It was not until fifteen years later, when people's hearts had softened, that specific commands to desist from adultery and drinking were revealed in the Qur'an. Aisha makes the point that if these commands had been revealed in the beginning, the Arabs would have stoutly refused to give up either adultery or drinking.

This shows that the Islamic Shariah was built up on the principle of gradualism. People's hearts had first of all to be touched, then their willingness to conform had to become apparent, and only then were the pronouncements of the shariah to be put into practice. Implementing the shariah does not mean using the whip or the gun. No good would ever come of such an imposition particularly on an unprepared society and would certainly not be in keeping with the methods favoured by the Prophet. No success can ever, in fact, be achieved by flouting his words of wisdom.

Pragmatism Instead of Idealism

In the Prophet's view, idealism was something to be striven for with reference to one's own thoughts and conduct, but he nevertheless felt that in one's dealings with others one had to resort to pragmatism. This was an important principle evolved by the Prophet, and his entire life serves as an illustration of it.

There was a notable instance of his using this approach when the Peace Treaty between the Muslims and the Quraysh was being drawn up. When the Prophet dictated these words: "This is from Muhammad, the Messenger of God," the Qurayshi delegate raised the objection that they did not believe in his prophethood, and demanded that the wording should be changed from Muhammad, the Messenger of God, to Muhammad, the son of Abdullah.

The Prophet realized that if he insisted upon retaining the words, 'Messenger of God.' the peace treaty might never be finalized. So he had the words 'Messenger of God' deleted, and in their place was written simply 'Muhammad, son of Abdullah.'

The great success achieved by the Prophet in Arabia owes much to this method of dealing with delicate situations. There are innumerable people in this world and everyone enjoys freedom. That is why no great success can be achieved here without adopting the ways of pragmatism.

The Prophet Muhammad, upon whom be peace, was undoubtedly a highly successful man. However, this extraordinary success was achieved through following certain high principles. I have attempted to deal here briefly with only some of these principles.

It is a well-known fact that the Prophet of Islam (PBUH) was the supremely successful man in the entire human history. But he was not just a hero, as Thomas Carlyle has called him. According to the Qur'an, he was a good example for all mankind. He has shown us the way of achieving supreme success in this world.

By studying the life of the Prophet we can derive those important principles which were followed by the Prophet. In short, the Prophet of Islam was a positive thinker in the full sense of the word. All his activities were result-oriented. He completely refrained from all such steps as may prove counter-productive. He always followed positive methods to achieve his goal.

1. First Principle: To begin from the possible

This principle is well explained in a saying of Aishah. She said: "Whenever the Prophet had to choose between two options, he always opted for the easier choice." (Al-Bukhari)

To choose the easiest option means to begin from the

possible, and one who begins from the possible will surely reach his goal.

2. Second Principle: To see advantage in disadvantage

In the early days of Mecca, there were many problems and difficulties. At that time, a guiding verse in the Qur'an was revealed. It said: "With every hardship there is ease, with every hardship there is ease." (94:5-6).

This means that if there are some problems, there are also opportunities at the same time. And the way to success is to ignore the problems and avail the opportunities.

3. Third Principle: To change the place of action

This principle is derived from the Hijrah. Hijrah was not just a migration from Mecca to Medina. It was to find a more suitable place for Islamic work, as history proved later on.

4. Fourth Principle: To make a friend out of an enemy

The prophet of Islam was repeatedly subjected to practices of antagonism by the unbelievers. At that time the Qur'an enjoined upon him the return of good for evil. And then, as the Qur'an added, "You will see your direst enemy has become your closest friend" (41:34).

It means that a good deed in return of a bad deed has a conquering effect over your enemies. And the life of the Prophet is a historical proof of this principle.

5. Fifth Principle: To turn minus into plus

After the Battle of Badr, about 70 of the unbelievers were taken as the prisoners of war. They were educated people. The Prophet announced that if any one of them would teach ten Muslim children how to read and write he would be freed. This was the first school in the history of Islam in which all of the students were Muslims, and all of the teachers were from the enemy rank. Here I shall quote a British orientalist who remarked about the Prophet of Islam: He faced adversity with the determination to wring success out of failure.

6. Sixth Principle: The power of peace is stronger than the power of violence

When Mecca was conquered, all of the Prophet's direst opponents were brought before him. They were war criminals, in every sense of the word. But the Prophet did not order to kill them. He simply said: "Go, you are free." The result of this kind behaviour was miraculous. They immediately accepted Islam.

7. Seventh Principle: Not to be a dichotomous thinker

In the famous Ghazwa of Muta, Khalid bin Walid decided to withdraw Muslim forces from the battlefield because he discovered that the enemy was unproportionately outnumbered. When they reached Medina, some of the Muslims received them by the word "O Furrar" (O deserters!) The Prophet said "No. They are Kurrar" (men of advancement)."

Those Medinan people were thinking dichotomously, either fighting or retreating. The Prophet said no. There is also a third option, and that is to avoid war and find a time to strengthen yourself. Now history tells us that the Muslims, after three years of preparation, advanced again towards the Roman border and this time they won a resounding victory.

8. Eighth Principle: To bring the battle in one's own favourable field

This principle is derived from the Ghazwa of Hudaibiyya. At that time, the unbelievers were determined to engage Muslims in fighting, because obviously they were in an advantageous position. But the Prophet, by accepting their conditions unilaterally, entered into a pact. It was a ten-year peace treaty. Until then, the meeting ground between Muslims and non-Muslims had been on the battlefield. Now the area of conflict became that of ideological debate. Within two years, Islam emerged as victorious because of the simple reason of its ideological superiority.

9. Ninth Principle: Gradualism instead of radicalism

This principle is well-established by a hadith of Al-Bukhari. Aishah says that the first verses of the Qur'an were related mostly to heaven and hell. And then after a long time when the people's hearts had softened, the specific commands to desist from adultery and drinking were revealed in the Qur'an.

This is a clear proof that for social changes, Islam advocates the evolutionary method, rather than the revolutionary method.

10. Tenth Principle: To be pragmatic in controversial matters

During the writing of Hudaibiyyah treaty, the Prophet dictated these words: "This is from Muhammad, the Messenger of God." The Qurayshi delegate raised objections over these words. The Prophet promptly changed the word and ordered to write simply Muhammad, son of Abdullah.

These were the principles through which the Prophet of Islam gained that success which has been recognized by historians as the supreme success.

In the end, I would like to repeat those ten principles of success:

1.   To begin from the possible
2.   To see advantage in disadvantage
3.   To change the place of action
4.   To make a friend out of an enemy
5.   To turn minus into plus
6.   The power of peace is stronger than the power of violence
7.   Not to be a dichotomous thinker
8.   To bring the battle in one's own favourable field
9.   Gradualism instead of radicalism
10. To be pragmatic in controversial matters

PART IV

The Policy of Peace in Islam
How to attain normalcy
in Jerusalem

According to the Prophet Muhammad, upon whom be peace, a believer is one with whom one can trust one's life and property. That is because Islam is a religion of peace. The Qur'an calls its way 'the paths of peace' (5:16). It describes reconciliation as the best policy, (4:128) and states quite plainly that God abhors disturbance of the peace (2:205).

Yet, in this world, for one reason or the other, peace remains elusive. Differences—political and apolitical— keep on arising between individuals and groups, Muslims and non-Muslims. Whenever people refuse to be tolerant of these differences, insisting that they be rooted out the moment they arise, there is bound to be strife. Peace, as a result, can never prevail in this world.

One recent example is the ever-recurring conflict over Jerusalem. Jerusalem is a very ancient, historic city with a unique value for all the millions of people of different religious persuasions who believe it to be their very own Sacred Place. Jerusalem is, indeed, a symbol and centre of inspiration for the three great Semitic religions of Judaism, Christianity and Islam. For Jews, it is a living proof of their ancient grandeur, and the pivot of their national history. For Christians, it is the scene of their Saviour's agony and triumph. For Muslims, it is the first halting place on the Prophet's mystic journey, and also the site of one of Islam's most sacred Shrines. Thus, for all three faiths, it is a centre of pilgrimage, while for Muslims it is the third holiest place of worship.

Now the question arises as to how, when it is a place of worship for all three religions, it can be freely accessible to all. How can the adherents of all the three religions have the opportunity there to satisfy their religious feelings?

Nowadays, all around us, we hear the slogan: "Jerusalem is ours." The raising of this slogan by different parties clearly shows that each one desires political supremacy for itself. All the three believe that without political dominance over this sacred city, they cannot worship God in the proper sense of the word.

If the condition for visiting this sacred place were that only that person or group could visit it who enjoyed political dominance there, Jerusalem would be turned from a place of peaceful worship into a battlefield. As political power can be wielded by only one religious group at a time, the other two groups, who are not in power, will constantly be in opposition to it. In this way, a place which should remain perfectly 'tranquil' will be eternally rent by clash and confrontation. As a result, not even the group in power will have the opportunity to perform its religious rites in peace.

This is indeed a very practical and important question which demands a serious rethinking. I would like to deal here briefly with the position of Islam in this matter.

The first indirect reference to Jerusalem appears in the 17th surah of the Qur'an. It says: 'Glory be to Him who made His Servant go by night from the Sacred Mosque to the distant Mosque, whose precincts We have blessed, that we might show him some of Our Signs' (17:1). Prior to the emigration in early 622, the Prophet Muhammad went on an extraordinary journey called Mi'raj (Ascension) in the history of Islam. Through God's unseen arrangement, this journey took the Prophet from Mecca to Jerusalem. There, according to the belief of the Muslims, he performed a prayer in congregation with all the Prophets who had been his forerunners at the holy site of al-Masjid al-Aqsa (al Bayt al-Maqdis).

Another reference to Jerusalem appears in one of the sayings of the Prophet recorded in all the six authentic books of Hadith with minor differences in wording. According to this tradition, there are only three mosques to which a journey may be lawfully made for the purpose of saying one's prayers—al-Masjid al-Haram of Mecca, al-Masjid al-Nabi of Medina and al-Masjid al-Aqsa of Jerusalem. (Certain traditions use the name Masjid Ilia for the Masjid al-Aqsa in Palestine.) Yet another tradition tells us that there is a far greater reward for praying in these three mosques than in any other mosque.

We learn, however, from the Qur'an that in no part of the world can political power be wielded indefinitely by the same nation or group: 'We bring these days to men by turns' (3:140). Given that power changes hands from time to time between different communities, how are believers to worship at al-Masjid al-Aqsa? Whereas each Muslim has a natural desire to enter this mosque and prostrate himself before God as the Prophet Muhammad and the other Prophets did.

According to the Qur'an, political power, by the very law of nature, cannot forever remain with one nation. In that case, if this act of worship is linked with the notion that a Muslim can receive God's blessings only when this land is under Muslim political rule, millions of Muslims would have had to bury this desire in their hearts and leave this world with this cherished desire unfulfilled, as it happened with the former Saudi king Faisal ibn Abdul Aziz (1906-1975). They would never have had, the unique experience of prostrating themselves before Almighty God at a place where the Prophet Muhammad, along with all the Prophets, had prostrated himself before his Lord.

What is the solution to this problem? Its solution lies in a practice (sunnah) of the Prophet Muhammad: to separate the religious from the political aspect of the matter. This would enable men of religion to solve the problem by applying what is called 'practical wisdom,' that is, to avoid the present problems and grasp the available opportunities. By following this process, they would be able to fulfill their cherished religious desire of which they have been denied unnecessarily so far. In the process, they would be able to avoid confrontational situations. Here are some telling examples of this sunnah of the Prophet.

1. The Prophet Muhammad emigrated from Mecca to Medina in July 622. For the first year and a half in Medina (i.e. till the end of 623) he and his companions prayed in the direction of al-Bayt al-Maqdis in Jerusalem. At the beginning of 624, the faithful, were enjoined, by Qur'anic revelation, to face in the direction of the Sacred Ka'ba at Mecca to say their prayers (2:144).

When this injunction regarding the Qiblah (direction of prayer) was revealed, 360 idols were still in position in the Ka'bah, at that time a long-established centre of polytheism. The presence of these idols must certainly have made Muslims feel reluctant to face in the direction of the Ka'bah at prayer time. How could believers in monotheism turn their faces towards what was, in effect, a structure strongly associated with polytheism? It is significant that along with the change of Qiblah came the injunction to treat this problem as a matter requiring patience, and not to hesitate in facing the Ka'bah: "O believers, seek assistance in prayer. God is with those who are patient" (2:153).

As history tells us, this state of affairs continued for six long years, till the conquest of Mecca (630) when the Ka'bah was cleared of idols. This establishes a very important principle of Islam which may be termed as Al-fasl bayn al-qaziyatayn, that is, the separation of two different facets of a problem from each other. According to this principle, the Ka'bah and the idols were given separate consideration. By remaining patient on the issue of the presence of the idols, believers were able to accept the Ka'bah as the direction for prayer.

2. Another such example is the above mentioned heavenly journey (Isra or Mi'raj) undertaken by the Prophet before the emigration in 622. At that juncture, Jerusalem was ruled by Iranians, that is to say, by non-Muslims. The Iranian ruler, Khusroe Parvez, attacked Jerusalem in 614, wresting it from the Romans, who had governed it since 63 B.C. This political dominance of the Iranian empire ended only when the Roman Emperor Heraclius defeated the Iranians and restored Roman rule over Jerusalem in 629.

This means that, before his emigration, the Prophet Muhammad entered Jerusalem on his Mi'raj journey to say his prayer at the Masjid al-Aqsa at a time when the city was under the rule of a non-Muslim king. From this we derive the very important sunnah of the Prophet that worship and politics practically belong to separate spheres, and, as such, should not be confused with one another.

3. The third example took place after the Hijrah in 629. At that time, Mecca was entirely under the domination of the idolatrous Quraysh. In spite of that, the Prophet and his companions came to Mecca from Medina to spend three days there to perform Umrah (the minor pilgrimage) and the circumambulation of the Ka'bah. This was possible solely because the Prophet did not mix worship with politics. If the Prophet had thought that Umra could be performed only when Mecca came under Muslim political rule, he would never have entered Mecca for worship along with his companions.

In the light of this sunnah of the Prophet, the solution to the present problem of Jerusalem lies in separating the issue of worship from that of political supremacy. Muslims belonging to Palestine, or any other country, should be able to go freely to Jerusalem in order to pray to God in the Aqsa Mosque. Worship should be totally disassociated from political issues.

To sum it up, the only practical solution to the problem of Jerusalem, in present circumstances, is to apply the above principle of Al-fasl bayn al-qaziyatayn to this matter, that is, to keep the two aspects of a controversial issue separate from one another. There is no other possible solution to the problem of Jerusalem. We ought to keep the political aspect apart from its religious aspect so that no ideological barrier comes in the way of worship by the people, and the faithful are able to go to Jerusalem freely

Limits of Tolerance

According to Voltaire, "Tolerance is a law of nature stamped on the heart of all men."

Nothing could be truer than this statement; tolerance is, indeed, a permanent law of nature. But it is not something which has to be externally imposed, for the human desire for tolerance is limitless. Just as truth and honesty are virtues, so is tolerance a virtue. And just as no one ever needs to ask for how long one should remain truthful and honest, so does one think of tolerance as having an eternal value. The way of tolerance should be unquestioningly adopted at all times as possessing superior merit.

A man who is intolerant is not a human being in the full sense of the expression. To become enraged at antagonism is surely a sign of weakness. Of course, there are many who do not want to recognise the principle of tolerance as being eternal, for, in conditions of adversity, the temptation to retaliate becomes too strong. The feelings of anger which accompany negative reaction must somehow be vented, and those who think and act in this way are keen to retain the illusion that, in hitting back, they are not doing anything unlawful.

Such thinking is quite wrong. In reality, when a man is enraged at anything which goes against his will, tolerance as a priority becomes paramount. Many men strive to become supermen. But the true superman is one who, in really trying situations, can demonstrate his super-tolerance. Just any act of antagonism does not give us the licence to be intolerant. Rather, such occasions call for greater tolerance than in normal circumstances. In everyday matter, where there is none of the stress and strain of opposition, no one has difficulty in being tolerant. It is only in extraordinary situations, fraught with conflict, that the truly tolerant man will prove his mettle.

On January 1st, 1995, the United Nations proclaimed 1995 as the "Year of Tolerance," saying that the ability to be tolerant of the actions, beliefs and opinions of others is a major factor in promoting world peace. The statement issued by the United Nations Educational, Scientific and Cultural Organisation, (UNESCO) on this occasion, emphasises that amidst the resurgence of ethnic conflicts, discrimination against minorities and xenophobia directed against refugees and asylum-seekers, tolerance is the only way forward. It pointed out that racism and religious fanaticism in many countries had led to many forms of discrimination and the intimidation of those who held contrary views. Violence against and intimidation of authors, journalists and others who exercise their freedom of expression, were also on the increase along with political movements which seek to make particular groups responsible for social ills such as crime and unemployment. Intolerance is one of the greatest challenges we face on the threshold to the 21st century, said the UNESCO Statement. Intolerance is both an ethnic and political problem. It is a rejection of the differences between individuals and between cultures. When intolerance becomes organised or institutionalised, it destroys democratic principles and poses a threat to world peace. (The Hindustan Times, January 1, 1995)

This proclamation of the U.N. is most apt and timely. The prime need of the world today is indeed tolerance.

One of the stark realities of life is that divergence of views does exist between man and man, and that it impinges at all levels. Be it at the level of a family or a society, a community or a country, differences are bound to exist everywhere. Now the question is how best unity can be forged or harmony brought about in the face of human differences.

Some people hold that the removal of all differences is the sine quanon for bringing about unity. But, this view is untenable, for the simple reason that, it is not practicable. You may not like the thorns which essentially accompany roses, but it is not possible for you to pluck out all the thorns and destroy them completely. For, if you pluck out one, another will grow in its place. Even if you run a bulldozer over all rosebushes, new plants will grow in their place bearing roses which are ineluctably accompanied by thorns. In the present scheme of things, roses can be had only by tolerating the existence of thorns. Similarly, a peaceful society can be created only by creating and fostering the spirit of tolerance towards diversities. In this world, unity is achievable only by learning to unite in spite of differences, rather than insisting on unity without differences. For total eradication of differences is an impossibility. The secret of attaining peace in life is tolerance of disturbance of the peace.

There is nothing wrong in diversity of opinions. In fact, this is a positive quality which has many advantages. The beauty of the garden of life is actually enhanced if the flower of unity is accompanied by the thorn of diversity.

An advantage flowing from this attitude is that it

builds character. If you are well-mannered towards those whose views are similar to yours, you may be said to exhibit a fairly good character. But, if you behave properly with those holding divergent views from you or who criticise you, then you deserve to be credited with having an excellent character.

In the same way, a society whose members hold identical views and never have any controversial discussions, will soon find itself in the doldrums. The intellectual development of the members of this society will be frozen, because personal evolution takes place only where the interaction of divergent thinking provides the requisite mental stimuli.

The adoption of a policy of tolerance in the midst of controversy and in the face of opposition is not a negative step. It is undoubtedly a positive course of action.

Divergence of views plays an important role in the development of the human psyche. It is only after running the intellectual gauntlet that a developed personality emerges. If, in a human society, this process ceases to operate, the development of character will come to a standstill.

Nobody in this world is perfect. If a man is endowed with some good qualities, he may be lacking in others. This is one of the reasons for differences cropping up between people. But, for life as a whole, this disparateness is actually a great blessing: the good points of one man may compensate for the shortcomings of another, just as one set of talents in one man may complement a different set in another. If people could only learn to tolerate others' differences, their very forebearance would become a great enabling factor in collective human development.

After 1947, when the first government of independent India was formed, two important leaders were included in it. One was Pandit Jawaharlal Nehru and the other was

Sardar Vallabh Bhai Patel. Pandit Nehru's westernized ideas were in great contrast to the orientalism of Sardar Patel. And this caused frequent differences of opinion between these two leaders. But this proved to be a boon for the nation, because with Pandit Nehru's abilities compensating for the shortcomings of Sardar Patel, and vice versa, the end result was one of an efficacious complementarity. The above is a good example of the difference between the respective natures and opinions of individuals essential for human development in general.

The habit of tolerance prevents a man from wasting his time and talent on unnecessary matters. When negatively affected by another's unpalatable behaviour, your mental equilibrium is upset, whereas when emotionally untouched by such behaviour, your mind will fully retain its equilibrium and, without wasting a single moment, you will continue to carry out your duties in the normal way. The policy of tolerance or forbearance enhances your efficacy, while intolerant behaviour reduces it.

Tolerance is not an act of compulsion. It is a positive principle of life, expressing the noble side of a man's character. The existence of tolerant human beings in a society is just like the blooming of flowers in a garden.

Islam: A Tolerant Religion

So far as Islam is concerned, it is an entirely tolerant religion. Islam desires peace to prevail in the world. The Qur'an calls the way of Islam 'the paths of Peace' (5:16). The state of peace can never prevail in a society if a tolerant attitude is lacking in the people. Tolerance is the only basis for peace; in a society where tolerance is absent, peace likewise will be non-existent.

Peace is the religion of the universe. Peace should, therefore, be the religion of man too, so that, in the words of Bible, the will of the Lord may be done on earth as it is in heaven (Matthew 6:10).

In a similar vein, the Qur'an tells us that: "The sun is not allowed to overtake the moon, nor does the night outpace the day. Each in its own orbit runs" (36:40).

When God created heaven and the earth, He so ordered things that each part might perform its function peacefully without clashing with any other part. For billions of years, therefore, the entire universe has been fulfilling its function in total harmony with His divine plan.

The universe is following this path of peace—which is known in science as the law of nature as it is imposed upon it by God, whereas man has to adopt this path of peace of his own free will. This has been expressed in the Qur'an in these words: "Are they seeking a religion other than God's, when every soul in heaven and earth has submitted to Him, willingly or by compulsion? To Him they shall all return" (3:83).

Peace is no external factor to be artificially imposed upon man. Peace is inherent in nature itself. The system of nature set up by God already rests on the basis of peace. If this system is not disrupted, it will continue to slay the course set for it by the Almighty. But the only way to keep humanity on the path of peace is to rid it of corruption. That is why the Qur'an enjoins: "And do not corrupt the land after it has been set in order" (7:85).

In order to preserve the peace, established by nature, from disruption, two important injunctions have been laid down by Islam. One, at the individual level, stresses the exercise of patience, and the other, at the social level, forbids taking the offensive.

1. Negative reaction on the part of the individual is the greatest factor responsible for disrupting peace in daily life. It repeatedly happens that in social life one experiences bitterness on account of others. On such occasions, if one

reacts negatively, the matter will escalate to the point of a head-on collision. That is why Islam repeatedly enjoins us to tread the path of patience. The Qur'an says: Surely the patient will be paid their wages in full without measure (39:10).

The reason for the rewards for patience being so great is that patience is the key factor in maintaining the desired system of God. In the words of the Qur'an the patient man is the helper of God (61:14).

2. The other injunction, designed to maintain peace in human society, forbids the waging of an offensive war. No one in Islam enjoys the right to wage war against another. There are no grounds on which this could be considered justifiable.

There is only one kind of war permitted in Islam and that is a defensive war. If a nation, by deviating from the principles of nature, wages war against another nation, defence in such circumstances, subject to certain conditions, is temporarily allowed.

To sum up, Islam is a religion of peace. The Arabic root of Islam, 'silm', means peace. The Qur'an says: '...and God calls to the home of peace' (10:25).

Peace is basic to all religions. Let us all strive then to establish peace in the world, for that is the bedrock on which all human progress rests.

Religious Harmony

What the world needs today—perhaps more than anything else—is an acceptable formula for the attainment of religious harmony. This being currently one of the most important topics under discussion, I shall attempt to present here, in brief, the Islamic viewpoint.

Let us begin with a verse of the Qur'an which reads:

> *He that chooses a religion other than Islam, it will not be accepted from him, and in the world to come he will be one of the lost (3:85).*

In the opinion of certain interpreters, this verse implies that salvation according to Islam is destined exclusively for Muslims. Islam thus appears to uphold the superiority of the Muslim community. But this is an out-of-context interpretation and is certainly not correct.

Let us take another verse of the Qur'an which serves as an explanation of the above-quoted verse. It states that:

> *Believers, Jews, Christians, and Sabeans—whoever believes in God and the Last Day and does what is right—shall be rewarded by their Lord; they have nothing to fear or to regret (2:62).*

This verse rules out the concept of community superiority for any given group: even Muslims have been bracketed here along with other religious groups. The content of this verse makes it very clear that salvation, by Islamic standards, depends upon the individual's own actions, and that it is not the prerogative of any group. No man or woman can earn his or her salvation by the mere fact of associating with a particular group. Salvation will be achievable only by a person who truly believes in God and the world hereafter, and who has given genuine proof in this life of having lived a life of right action.

Another important aspect of Islam is that it does not advocate belief in the manyness of reality; on the contrary, it stresses reality's oneness. That is, according to Islam, reality is one, not many. That is why, in describing monotheism, the Qur'an states:

> Such is God, your rightful Lord. That which is not true
> must needs be false. How then can you turn away from
> Him? (10:32)

This verse makes it clear that monotheism (i.e. one Lord being the Creator, Sustainer and object of worship) is the only truth. All other paths lead one away from, rather than towards the truth. The fact that certain religious thinkers believe in the manyness of reality is of no concern to Islam. With oneness as its ideal, it cannot accept manyness even as a hypothesis.

Both of the above points—(a) the oneness of Absolute Reality, and (b) Salvation as the prerogative of the true believer in this oneness—form a major part of Islamic ideal. Just being born into a certain group or community, or associating oneself with others of similar persuasions, does not entitle one to salvation, be one a Muslim or a non-Muslim.

Now let us deal with the fact that; in practice, different kinds of religious groups do exist. Then, given the various kinds of differences separating them, let us consider, how to bring about harmony between them.

One solution commonly advocated is to spread the conviction that all religions are essentially one: that they are simply diverse paths leading to a common destination. Islam, however, does not accept this view and, in any case, experience has shown that repeated attempts to bring about harmony on this basis have been a failure. The Emperor Akbar attempted to achieve harmony by state enforcement of his newly formed religion, 'Din-e-Ilahi;' Dr Bhagwan Das spent the best part of his life producing a one-thousand page book titled Essential Unity of All Religions; Mahatma Gandhi (1869-1948) attempted to spread this ideal at the national level by a countrywide movement whose slogan was 'Ram Rahim ek hai,' meaning Ram and Rahim were one and the same. But events have shown us that all failed in their attempts to achieve the goal of religious harmony.

Islam's approach to the entire problem is much more realistic in that it accepts ideological differences. Once having accepted these differences, it then advocates the policy of tolerance and respect for one another in everyday dealings. This is on a parallel with the principle expressed in the English saying, 'Let's agree to disagree.'

In this connection, one of the commands of the Qur'an is that, in principle, 'there shall be no compulsion in religion' (2:256). At another place it declares that 'you have your religion and I have mine' (109:6). It was as a result of this commandment that, when the Prophet Muhammad migrated to Medina, he issued a declaration reaffirming his acceptance of the religion of Muslims for the Muslims and the religion of Jews for the Jews.' In order to perpetuate the atmosphere of mutual harmony, the Qur'an commands the Muslims in their dealings with unbelievers not to 'revile (the idols) which they invoke besides Allah, lest in their ignorance they should spitefully revile Allah.'

This principle formulated by Islam is best described not as religious harmony, but as harmony among religious people. This is a principle whose utility is a matter of historical record. It is evident that in the past as well as in the present, wherever religious harmony has existed, it has been based on unity despite differences, rather than on unity without differences. It is not based on agreeing to agree, but on agreeing to disagree.

One extremely revolutionary example of this principle is to be found in the life of the Prophet Muhammad. It concerns the conference of three religions which was held in the Prophet's own mosque in Medina. This conference is described by Muhammad Husain Haykal in his book, The Life of Muhammad:

> The three scriptural religions thus confronted one another in Madinah. The delegation entered with the Prophet into public debate and these were soon joined by the Jews, thus resulting in a tripartite dialogue between Judaism, Christianity and Islam. This was a truly great congress which the city of Yathrib had witnessed. In it, the three religions which today dominate the world and determine its destiny had met, and they did so for the greatest idea and the noblest purpose.

Although Islam believes, in the oneness of reality it lays equal stress on the practice of tolerance in everyday dealings, even if it means going to the extent of permitting

non-Muslims to come to an Islamic place of worship for
religious discussion, and if it is time for their prayers
letting them feel free to perform their worship according
to their own ways in the mosque itself.

Tolerance has been the rule throughout the history of
Islam. It has, in fact, been one of the main underlying
causes of its successful dissemination. Here I quote from
the Encyclopaedia Britannica:

> *Islam achieved astonishing success in its first phase.*
> *Within a century after the Prophet's death in a.d. 632*
> *(the early generations of Muslims) it had brought a*
> *large part of the globe—from Spain across central Asia*
> *to India—under a new Arab Muslim empire.*

And this is the part which I wish particularly to stress:

> *Despite these astonishing achievements other religious*
> *groups enjoyed full religious autonomy (9/912).*

Now the complicating factor is that when any religion
having reached this stage of antiquity has secured a sacred
place in the hearts of its believers, it becomes impossible
to bring about any changes in it. Efforts to bring about a
change can produce a new religion, but they can never
succeed in changing the old religion. There are many
examples of such failures in the past.

A very important point from the practical point of
view is that although the necessity to bring about harmony
among the different religions is not a newly-felt imperative,
endeavours towards that end are still only in the formative
stages. If progress towards that goal has been slow of
attainment, it is because of the established positions which
ancient religions have secured in the hearts of their
followers, simply by virtue of their antiquity. Trying to
bring about changes in these religions per se has never

brought about harmony, because instead of old religions being brought closer together by this process, they have developed rather into new religions, a process which has either left the problem of disharmony unsolved or has further aggravated it. There are many examples of such abortive efforts in the past.

In view of this historical reality, it is clear that the suggestions made by Islam as to how to produce harmony among the different religions is the only viable solution. Any alternative suggestion, however attractive it might appear, would be either impracticable or counter-productive.

Once, when discussing this point with me, a religious scholar said, 'We have been attempting to bring about interreligious harmony for the last one hundred years, but the results have been quite dismal. It would seem that there are insurmountable obstacles in the way.'

I replied that the goal we want to attain is certainly a proper one; it is simply that the strategy we employ is impracticable. Religious harmony is without doubt a desirable objective. But it cannot be achieved by attempting to alter people's beliefs—a policy advocated by more than one scholar in this field. The only way to tackle the problem is to encourage people to show respect for others' beliefs and to be humanitarian at all times in their dealings with adherents of other religions. It is vital to realize that it is quite possible to inculcate this attitude without in any way tampering with long-cherished credos. It should never be conceded that the goal of religious harmony is unattainable simply because people's beliefs differ from each other. It is certainly a possibility provided that it is seen as a matter of practical strategy and not as a pretext for making ideological changes.

'Practical strategy' is something which people regularly resort to in matters of their daily existence. As such, it is a known and acceptable method of solving the problem. Since no new ground has to be broken, either for the religious scholar or for the common man, it should be a very simple matter for people to extend their everyday activity, within their own sphere of existence, to include an honest and sincere effort towards global religious harmony. It is simply a question of having the will and the foresight to do so.

PART V

Towards a Non-Violent World

Though the history of the non-violent movement is a very long one, historians concede that "the most massive and historically effective example of non-violent activism was that of the movement organized by Mahatma Gandhi" (13/850).

India can be justly proud that it was in this country, under the leadership of Mahatma Gandhi, that for the first time in human history a non-violent movement culminated in such resounding success.

The first target for Mahatma Gandhi was to usher in peaceful political change throughout the country. This ambition was fulfilled in 1947. Mahatma Gandhi's second target was to bring about social change on the basis of non-violence. But before he could achieve his second target, he was tragically removed from the scene of action.

Now our greatest need is to fulfill Mahatma Gandhi's mission. After political change we have to bring about social change in our country through Gandhi Andolan, that is, a non-violent movement. If India could be successful on this front, it would undoubtedly find itself in a position to give the lead to the entire world.

There is only one way of exploiting the non-violent method for the reform of a society—and that is, to bring about a change in the thinking of the individual, who is the basic unit of society.

Someone has rightly observed that all violence is born in the mind and that it can be ended in the mind itself. For instance, during the second world war, Japan was burning to revenge itself on America. They said that America had devastated their town of Hiroshima, so they would devastate America. Although Japan's air force had been badly hit, its army was still intact, and its officers were bent on vengeance. At that juncture certain intellectuals in Japan pointed out that if America had destroyed their Hiroshima, they had already destroyed America's Pearl Harbour. In this way they were on a par. The score was even.

Due to this timely guidance, the Japanese came to rethink their position, and, abandoning the path of confrontation with America, and opting instead for the path of adjustment with it; in so doing, they were tremendously successful.

The truth is that intellectual awakening is the only way to produce a non-violent world. This is, without doubt, a long and laborious struggle. But we have no other alternative. I have myself been experimenting for the last 25 years in this field and my experience has been successful to a satisfactory extent.

After giving the matter a great deal of thought, I have come to the conclusion that, in most instances, violence is the result of misguided thinking. The day you succeed in putting an end to such thought, violence will of itself disappear.

Take the case, for example, of communal riots in India. In this matter I have done considerable work among the Muslims, having found that in most of the cases communal riots result from this erroneous way of thinking. I have always taken great pains to make them understand, for example, that when the procession are being led through the streets by other communities, the choice before them is not, as they imagine, either to tolerate the procession or to disrupt and stop it completely, but between tolerance of the procession and communal riots.

A procession is little more than a nuisance of a temporary nature. So one should simply bear with it so that riots resulting in human death and destruction do not ensue.

After December 6, 1992, surprisingly few communal riots have taken place. The credit for this goes to our mission. Had the people's minds not been prepared by our mission, terrible riots involving great numbers of people would have ensued subsequent to December. 6.

When there is violence, at whatever level and in whatever field, the basic question is at all events of the individual. And an individual is always governed by his thinking. That is why, if we have to make a non-violent world for a peaceful society, there is only one way, and that is by using educative method to convert people's thinking from violence to non-violence, and to enable them to seek the solution to matters of controversy through peaceful means. They must learn to understand the value of tolerance and avoidance as opposed to intolerance and confrontation. It is from such intellectual awareness alone that a non-violent world and a peaceful society can be constructed.

Co-existence of Religions in India

In India, there has always been co-existence of religions in an ideal form. With a few minor exceptions, a number of religions, notwithstanding their different sets of beliefs, have always flourished here together in complete harmony. It is no exaggeration to say that the example set by India in this sphere is quite outstanding.

The most ancient religion of India, dating back to pre-historic times, is Hinduism. Then, in the fifth century BC, a new religion, Buddhism, was founded by Gautam Buddha. During roughly the same period a religion known as Jainism was founded by Mahavira. Both of the latter religions were originally separate from Hinduism, there having been some initial rift. But, ultimately, Buddha came to be recognized as an incarnation, or avtar of Vishnu. Similarly, Jainism became a sect of Hinduism.(EB 8/906).

About fifteen hundred years ago, Christians came to India where they propagated Christianity among the Indian people. Later, Muslims ventured on to Indian soil and, with their advent, Islam began to spread here. But, leaving aside certain exceptional incidents, no clash or confrontation took place between Hinduism, Christianity and Islam.

The underlying reason for this is quite specific. It is the remarkable flexibility of their beliefs and teachings. This, indeed, is the basis for the spirit of accommodation which has made possible the continuing co-existence of the various religious groups in this country.

So far as Hinduism, the religion of the majority, is concerned, it serves as the ultimate example of religious flexibility, with its unique concept of the manyness of reality. Its credo amounts to saying, 'I am right and you are also right.' It is, thanks to this particular belief that Hindus have such deep respect in their hearts for other religions. For them, all religions are manifestations of the same Truth.

Although neither Christianity nor Islam entertain this plural concept of Truth, they both subscribe to another tenet which is also conducive to harmony, namely, respect for other religions. Christianity and Islam both stress the need to respect other religious groups and to show proper regard for them, irrespective of the circumstances.

Just as religious co-existence is valued in Hinduism, so also is it valued in Christianity and Islam. If any differences arise, they do so as a matter of rationale, and not of actual practice. That is, the goal of co-existence is achieved in Hinduism through co-recognition, while in Christianity and Islam, it is achieved through mutual esteem.

In this way, even with conflicting sets of beliefs (that is, the manyness of reality and the oneness of reality) the desired goal of co-existence is a fully established fact. The basis of this co-existence in Hinduism is the belief in a common, underlying Truth, while in Christianity and

Islam, this goal is achieved through tolerance. That is to say that in one case this co-existence is found at a conceptual level, while, in the other, it is at a practical level. Whatever its intellectual sources may be, the end result—co-existence—is the same.

There are many examples of this kind of practical agreement within the fold of Hinduism itself. For instance, a vegetarian Hindu and a non-vegetarian Hindu adhere to different principles, but for practical reasons, they live happily together without ever coming into conflict with one another.

In recent years, India has seen various clashes and confrontations in the name of religion, and the country's image has apparently been affected by these incidents. But this has been due less to the actual points at issue than to the media's sensational coverage of them.

For instance, in 1985, a case was filed in the Calcutta High Court by a Hindu, asking that a ban be imposed on the Qur'an. This incident was given undue emphasis in media coverage, but its outcome only served as a further proof that religious co-existence is to be found in India in its ideal form, for not only was his case dismissed by the court, but his action was condemned by all national institutions and by the whole of the Hindu community.

Another instance of the refusal of the Hindu community to condone a show of disrespect for Islam was in the now infamous case of the Babari Masjid being razed to the ground. There had been discord over this mosque for a long period of time until, finally, on December 6, 1992, a group of Hindus took it upon themselves to demolish it.

It is important to understand that this tragedy took place because of certain misguided policies of political leaders and not because of religious intolerance. That is

why no notable Hindu or non-Hindu ever came forward
to justify the demolition of the Babri Masjid. And that is
also why—with the exception of the Babri Masjid—
approximately 350,000 mosques in India are still intact.
They are all safe and secure, and are functioning as centres
of religious worship and practice. Another point worth
noting is that Justice P.K. Bahri has ruled in his 340-page
verdict that the demolition of the disputed structure at
Ayodhya was not pre-planned. (The Times of India , June
9, 1993)

Here I should like to emphasize that one religion
versus another religion is quite a different matter from
one community versus another community. So far as
religion in itself is concerned, it is a fact that religious co-
existence has always been found in its ideal form
throughout the history of India.

It is interesting to note that prior to 1947 in undivided
India, it was non-Muslims who were the biggest publishers
and distributors of Islamic literature. It is even more
interesting that in divided India, it is still the non-Muslims
who are to the fore in this field.

There are, of course, examples of religious intolerance,
but these have always been the result of discord between
two communities rather than between two religions. It
has sometimes happened that members of one religious
community have entered into dispute with members of
another community over matters relating to their own
individual or group interest (as opposed to religious
interests) and then used arguments garbed in religious
terminology to support their standpoint. Similarly,
members of a certain community have been known to
raise an issue publicly to serve their own political or
material ends, again in the process using religion to

further their own, individual, selfish interests. This is not religion. It is the exploitation of religion.

This kind of exploitation is always against the spirit of religion. That is why it cannot be continued indefinitely. It remains limited in its sphere and duration.

In modern India, slogans are shouted advocating the establishment of the Hindu Rashtra. In a plural society, such slogans are obviously against the spirit of co-existence, and, as such, are considered a danger by certain sections of the public. But I personally do not attach any importance either to them or to the present movement launched in the name of establishing the Hindu Rashtra. Those who fear for their future should take heart from the historic outcome of Mahatma Gandhi's pre-1947 independence movement, launched in the name of Ram Rajya, for, after independence, the system introduced was not that of Ram Rajya, but of secular Rajya.

With 75 per cent of the Indian population being either illiterate, or semi-literate, political leaders regularly make use of religious slogans to secure the public vote. But the roots of co-existence and mutual tolerance are so strong, and go so deep, that I am fully convinced that politics of this kind will never exert any profound or lasting effect on Indian society. Such slogans, which are, in essence, more political than religious, will never succeed in disturbing the religious harmony of India.

Creating Harmony Amidst Cultural Conflict

There is no denying the fact that cultural conflict does exist in reality. However, this is a blessing in disguise. Conflict between different cultures has always existed in human history. The only thing new about this phenomena in our times is that the modern means of communication have greatly accelerated the pace of this process.

The second point I should like to make is that cultural conflict per se poses no danger. It rather denotes a healthy process. Arnold Toynbee's theory that challenges act as a spur to take the nations forward, applies to cultural conflict too. Challenges in fact are the only ladder to the ongoing progressive journey of human history.

In ancient time, the confrontation of Roman and non-Roman culture resulted in the emergence of Muslim nations, bringing the history forward. Afterwards, Muslim and non-Muslim culture, came into conflict resulting in the emergence of renaissance in Europe. History further moved forward.

In the twentieth century European and non-European cultures faced challenges. As a result of which the USA emerged on the scene with the greatest of progress ever made in history.

However this is in no way the final phase in human history. Now the collision is taking place between American and non-American culture which would result in a better, more advanced culture, and it is quite possible that this might be Indian or Asian culture.

The actual task to be performed by India and other under-developed countries is not to engage themselves in protest against the so-called cultural invasions. What is more important for us is to devote our attention to educating our people. Increasing the percentage of literacy among the people amounts to making them an aware, enlightened people. Once we have managed to make them an enlightened people, it is quite possible that those who are lagging behind today may become pioneers of a new cultural age, as has often taken place in history.

Solidarity and Islam

Solidarity means "unity of feeling and action among different individuals." Thus defined, it is a spirit truly worth fostering and, in this, religion has a major role to play. In fact, there can be no solidarity without religion. Being of the view that whenever religion is a true, living force, solidarity will naturally ensue, I should now like to present the Islamic viewpoint on this subject.

Religion, as summed up in Islamic teachings, is basically a matter of loving God and wishing other human beings well. Of the former, the Qur'an says, "The love of God is stronger in the faithful." (2:165) Of the latter, the Qur'an has to say: "Those who believe, enjoin patience and enjoin mercy." (90:17)

This is basic to the teachings of all religions and sums up the principal tenets of Islam. It is quite apparent that when human relationships come under the influence of such teachings, solidarity will, of itself, emerge as a psychological necessity, even amongst those who at the outset have little sense of fellow-feelings. Despite partial differences, they will come closer to one another. They will become friends.

Another important feature of Islam is that it reminds us of the biological truth that all human beings are God's family. All human beings are Adam's progeny. This means that, in the Islamic view, despite superficial differences, all human beings are blood brothers. When it is the aim of Islam to inculcate fellow-feeling among its followers, the believer will then have nothing but brotherly love for others. And where there is brotherly love, mutual solidarity will, of necessity, prevail.

My studies of Islam and other religions have made it plain to me that the difference between one religion and another lies in the diversity of beliefs about the great, unseen reality. This is an important point, but what is even more important is that, in so far as the human codes of ethics pertaining to our daily lives are concerned, there is no special difference between the world's great religions.

While the concept of God may vary from religion to religion, there is no fundamental difference over issues such as justice and fair dealing, mutual esteem and good, social relationships. This being so, when people are sincere adherents of true religion, the question of their coming with conflict with others simply does not arise. Real differences became apparent only when concepts of correct human behaviour differ radically from person to person. For instance, some believe in exploiting others, while others believe in coming to the assistance of suffering humanity.

In the face of such contradictory moral values, it is more than likely that there will be clashes. But as I have said earlier, no such differences in ethical values exist between the various religions. Differences arise in human transactions only when no true religious spirit is present.

Conversely, the existence of true religious spirit guarantees the absence of dissension.

To conclude, the criterion by which all men and all things are judged in Islam is the Qur'an. This means that Muslims are judged, and will continue to be judged by Islam, and not vice versa. If, in a Muslim society, there is no feeling of brotherhood for, or solidarity with the adherents of other faiths, this will be a sure indication that in that society there is a complete absence of the true spirit of Islam.

Progress in
Inter-Religious Dialogue

Religious differences have always existed between people. That is why interreligious dialogue has been found in one form or the other since ancient times. Fourteen hundred years ago the Prophet of Islam held in Medina a three-religion conference—in modern terminology, a trialogue—to exchange views on religious issues.

Such attempts have repeatedly been made in history. The circumstances that unfolded following the second world war led the Christian Church, in particular, to pay great attention to this matter. Through its continuous efforts dialogues of this nature are regularly being held in various countries, between Muslims and Christians in particular. I too have had the occasion to participate in several of these dialogues.

These efforts have borne fruit, at least partially. For instance, it is as a result of these efforts that on the one hand, a Church has appeared once again in Ben Ghazi (Libya) while on the other, a mosque has been built in Rome for the first time in recent history.

If the Qur'an is consulted with this point in view, we

find two main principles on which to hold dialogues. One is derived from this verse of the Qur'an:

> Say: O People of Book, Let us come to a word common
> to us and you that we will worship none but God (3:64).

The first and foremost principle for any dialogue held to discuss two or more religions is to strive to find a mutual basis for peaceful co-existence.

It is a fact that finding a common ground in secular matters is comparatively easy, for nothing is held as sacred in secularism. On the contrary everything acquires a sacred character in religion. That is why it becomes the most difficult task to find a basis for agreement in religious matters. However, despite all difficulties, we must continue our efforts, peacefully, irrespective of the results.

The second principle given by the Qur'an is purely a matter of pragmatism. That is, matters should be settled on practical grounds by avoiding their theoretical aspects. This principle is derived from this verse of the Qur'an:

> To you your religion and to me mine (109:6).

This principle is generally referred to, in today's context as religious co-existence. This means that whenever common grounds for agreement between two or more parties can not be arrived at on an ideological basis, then the way of practical co-existence must be adopted.

The Community of Saint Egidio provides a good example of a continuing dialogue of this nature. This promotes interaction on a mass scale between adherents of different religions. In view of its vastness it may be rightly termed a super dialogue. The religious meet held under the auspices of the Community of Saint Egidio on a large scale each year makes a considerable contribution towards the achievement of the goal targetted by interreligious dialogue.

Here I would like to add another point. We should not judge our efforts in this matter only by the results of meetings held in the name of formally arranged interreligious dialogue. The truth is that "interreligious dialogue" is not now limited to specific meetings held in the field of religion. It has rather assumed the form of a vast historical process—spontaneous, ongoing and perhaps never fully recorded. Negotiation in controversial matters is in tune with the spirit of the age. Today, it has permeated all walks of national as well as international life.

Modern industrial revolution and modern communication have added such vast dimensions to human relations that now the entire world has been converted into a global village. People of various persuasions are coming closer, on a universal scale. This interaction serves as an on-going dialogue of an informal nature. In this way with distances narrowed, the confrontational attitude now gives way to compromise.

Interaction in itself is an unproclaimed dialogue. When, as a result of circumstances, interaction between people of different persuasions increases, the purpose of the dialogue is served on its own.

Today, in educational institutions, offices, and factories, in travel, on playgrounds and in national and international activities, adherents of different religious traditions are meeting one another on a scale hitherto unwitnessed.

In the course of this continuous and vast interaction, for the first time in human history, people seem less like strangers to one another. A great gap has been bridged. People are learning one another's languages. They are becoming familiar with one another's culture. Making concessions to one another has become a need of the people themselves.

These factors have brought people closer right across the world. And it is a psychological truth that closeness and interaction in themselves serve the purpose of a practical dialogue. In this way, a natural dialogue has come into existence and has become an on-going process at all times and in all places.

Probably the most signal result of this historical process is that after a long intellectual struggle religious intolerance has been universally rejected. Religious intolerance has now been replaced with complete religious freedom. Today under auspices of the United Nations all the nations of the world have signed the universal declaration of human rights.

In accordance with this declaration religious freedom has been accepted as the natural birth-right of all human beings. As opposed to practices in ancient times, no one now enjoys the right to persecute anyone on the basis of religion. This is the change which has confined the sphere of religious difference to peaceful negotiation.

The effects of this can be seen in all walks of life, whether religious or secular. Every one of us, consciously or unconsciously, plays a part in making religious co-existence a reality.

Interfaith dialogue becoming a part of the historical process holds great promise for us, as in this case its success is assured. This is how every great revolution of history has got under way. Whenever a movement goes beyond the stage of individual or group efforts and joins the historical process itself, then the continuity of that movement is ensured and ultimately nothing can stop it reaching its destination.

In short, inter-religious dialogue had its beginnings in

individual interaction, paving the way for discussions held in religious gatherings. Ultimately the time came when it became a part of a world movement. Now, if the course of events is any indication, God willing, that day too will dawn when the world is no more ridden with religious disputes, and we are able to live in a peaceful and harmonious world.

PART VI

Islam: The Ideological Superpower

Muslims number more than one billion today. If you go round the world to study the minds of Muslims inhabiting various regions, you will probably come to the conclusion that Muslims all over the world share the feeling that the history of Islam has reached an impasse. Despite enormous sacrifices, no way out is in sight.

It is our firm belief that Islam offers guidance at all times and in all situations. Therefore, it must certainly be able to offer us clear guidance on the present state of affairs. The history of Islam does indeed provide us with two very clear examples of bringing into play the *da'wah* power of Islam.

1. The first guiding example recorded in the early period of Islamic history is that of *Sulh-e-Hudaybiyya*. As we all know, the Prophet of Islam was compelled to migrate from Mecca to Medina. The majority of Muslims followed him. Consequently Medina became a centre of Muslims. However, later events took a more serious turn. The opponents of Islam now started armed onslaughts against the Muslims. Yet after several full-scale wars and

many minor armed conflicts, the balance failed to tip on any side. Apparently the history of Islam had reached an impasse.

At this critical juncture, according to the Qur'an, the Prophet of Islam was shown the straight path in this matter (48:3-4). This meant creating an atmosphere conducive to peaceful *da'wah* work by ceasing armed conflicts altogether. Accordingly, the Prophet in the 19th year of his prophethood entered into a peace treaty with his Arab opponents. This step put an end to the state of war. This event is referred to in the history of Islam as *Sulh-e-Hudaybiyya*. This peace treaty changed the area of encounter between Islam and its rivals from the battlefield to the *Da'wah* field.

This peaceful activism brought incredible revolutionary results. The power of peace proved itself far superior to the power of war. This treaty rendered possible a widespread interaction between Muslims and the opposing group in a normal atmosphere. In this way, the peace treaty cleared the path for the direct propagation of Islam to take place. The opponents came to accept Islam in such great numbers, that ultimately, by numerical power alone, Islam became the victor.

According to Imam al-Zuhari, Sulh-e-Hudaybiyya was the greatest victory in the history of Islam. Prior to this whenever Muslims and their rivals had encountered one another, fighting had ensued. But after the reconciliation, the state of war ended and peace prevailed. Now former antagonists began meeting one another in a normal, tension-free atmosphere. This interaction naturally led to an exchange of ideas. Whenever anyone heard anything of Islam that he found appealing, he would, without fail, enter its fold. That is why, in a mere two years after the signing of Sulh-e-Hudaybiyya, such a large number of people entered the fold of Islam as had never before been witnessed (*Al-Bidayah wa al-Nihayah*, vol. 4, p. 170).

This great increase in terms of numbers made Islam a majority religion in Arabia, which greatly facilitated its dominance throughout the land.

2. The second well-known example of the caravan of Islam having reached an impasse came about with the emergence of the brute force of the Tartars in the first half of the thirteenth century. Muslim power was almost completely destroyed by it. It seemed as though the journey of Islam had once again reached a point from which there could be no further advancement.

At exactly that point in time, the ideological power of Islam made its appearance. Muslims, being in no position to take up arms, re-channelized their energies by silently engaging themselves in peaceful da'wah work among the victorious Tartars. This act of da'wah verified the dictum of the Qur'an that, through da'wah, the opponents of Islam would become its supporters and friends (41:34).

Historians have acknowledged this event in quite clear terms. Philip K. Hitti, for instance, remarks, in his famous book, The History of the Arabs:

> "The religion of the Muslims had conquered where their arms had failed" (p. 488)

3. Now in the twentieth century the history of Islam appears once again to have reached an impasse. Enormous numbers of sacrifices on our part have yet to succeed in taking forward the caravan of Islam.

According to al-Imam Malik, the state of affairs of the Muslim Ummah will be reformed only by following the same course of action as that followed by the Muslims of the first phase in order to ameliorate their situation. In the light of this observation, it can be safely said that we must once again opt for this tested method of the past. We must take such steps as will put an end to the hostility prevailing between Muslims and non-Muslims. This would result in a normal situation in which peaceful interaction between Muslims and non-Muslims could fruitfully take place. Hudaybiyya symbolises the greatness of the power of peace as against the power of war. Today, once again, we need to follow a course of action which will create a similar set of circumstances.

As soon as this happens, the ideological power of Islam will at once appear in its full force—which is undoubtedly eternally invincible. Afterwards the virtues of Islam will begin reaching people automatically through exchange and interaction. Then it will also be possible to perform da'wah work properly. Under the influence of their own nature people will start joining the ranks of Islam. And there is no doubt about it that the greatest strength for any group depends upon its manpower.

Muslims can be weakened and subjugated at any point in time. But Islam is an ideological superpower forever. It has the capacity to conquer the greatest power on earth through da'wah. It is the need of the hour to produce conditions, on a universal scale, conducive to the dissemination of the word of God. It is necessary to bring into play the ideological power of Islam in order that da'wah work may be set in motion in the full sense of the word. And then, certainly, Islam will emerge as the dominant and conquering force, and Muslims of the world too will receive their place of honour and glory along with Islam.

Western Civilization and Islam

According to Sahih al-Bukhari the Prophet of Islam (PBUH) once observed: God will strengthen this religion through the wicked as well as the good. This hadith is of great significance so far as the art of thinking is concerned. It points to the error of dichotomous thinking, the tendency to see everything in terms of black and white. It implies that while people may fall into one of two categories—the good or the bad. They may also fall into a third category, i.e. that of potential supporters of Islam. That is, an individual may fall into the category of the good, yet still possess a third quality, i.e., that of enjoying a position to support the believers, in one way or another.

The outcome of the treaty of Hudaybiyya provides a practical example of the success of broader thinking in the early history of Islam. Apparently the Prophet's opponents were not pro-Islam. Therefore, the Muslims in general, because of the limitations in their thinking, mistakenly categorised them as enemies of Islam. But thanks to his divine wisdom, the Prophet did not fall into the error of regarding them as such. For he knew that a third possibility also existed. It was the latent potential of Da'wah. Therefore, the Prophet decided to open a door which had been closed to Da'wah by entering into a peace treaty with his opponents. Consequently, the possibilities of da'wah activism began taking shape and within a short period of two years the entire history of Islam was transformed.

To my way of thinking, the case of Western Civilization and Islam exactly parallels that of the Hudaybiyya situation in modern times. Muslims have once again fallen prey to limitations of dichotomous thinking in these matters. Since western civilization does not appear to them to be friendly to Islam, they tend to regard it as an enemy of Islam. Matters have so escalated that a section of Islamic thinkers have even taken to calling western civilization a manifestation of Dajjal.

If we could extricate ourselves from this rigid pattern of thought we would find that western civilization, was neither friendly nor hostile to Islam, but rather—in the words of hadith—a potential supporter of Islam.

Today, we are once again in need of divine wisdom adopted on the eve of Hudaybiyya. If we could but think in the same way as the Prophet did on that occasion, history would certainly repeat itself. Out of unfavourable circumstances, favourable possibilities would emerge, and by being able to exploit these possibilities, we would be able to build a new history of Islam.

Led by their political and economic interests, the upholders of western civilization follow many policies which are detrimental to the collective good of Muslims. This is an indisputable fact. In reality this has nothing to do with any enmity towards Islam. It is simply due to the imperatives of economic competition. The affairs of this world being based on the principle of competition, such events have always taken place and will continue to do so in the near and distant future. So what we must do is accept these things as a part of nature and turn our full attention to seeking out alternative possibilities in order to exploit them for our own purposes.

Such possibilities do exist for us inspite of all the apparently adverse circumstances in which we strive to perpetuate our Islamic heritage.

The hadith which mentions Dajjal appearing close to the time of Doomsday is doubtless correct, but certainly it does not apply to modern western civilization.

There is another hadith which would more correctly apply to the case of western civilization. In this the Prophet has made the prediction that close on Doomsday, the message of Islam will enter every hut or mansion.

The truth is that western civilization has emerged as a supporting factor in the divine scheme of Idkhal-e-Kalimah (the communication of the word of God to all human beings). The hadith pertaining to Dajjal has thus no direct bearing whatsoever on western civilization.

For this prediction to be fulfilled many contributory factors were required—factors which had never hitherto existed. It is western civilization alone which has provided for the first time in human history all those means and resources which were necessary for the realization of this process of Idkhal-e-kalimah (global communication of the divine message).

In this way, according to the words of hadith, the case of Western civilization is one neither of friendliness nor of hostility. It falls rather into a third category—that of supportiveness.

Here I would like to mention in brief a few examples of this supportive nature to serve as a practical explanation of this matter.

1. The first and foremost requirement for the performance of the mission of Idkhal-e-kalimah is the provision of a system of global communication. It is an acknowledged fact that the cultural revolution of the west is the first event in human history to have placed at our disposal such a worldwide system of communication—a prerequisite for the realization of Islamic goals.

2. The second requirement essential to facilitating this task was complete religious freedom. In the absence of religious freedom, successful communication of the desired nature had never been possible. Now western civilization has brought into being an era in which for the first time in human history freedom of religion has come to be accepted as a sacred human right. This is one of its greatest gifts to humanity.

3. In order to spread the word of God on a universal scale, an unlimited amount of wealth was required. It is through western civilization that the Muslim nations have been able, albeit indirectly, to secure this wealth. For it was people from the West who first discovered the wealth of petrol abounding in Muslim countries. It was again these very people who, by ushering in the modern machine age, gave petrol the status of a precious commodity. This wealth thus acquired has enabled the Muslims of today to spread their campaign throughout the entire world, regardless of the cost.

4. Another very important supporting factor pertains to the principle of free enquiry developed by the west. This principle of free enquiry was extended by them even to religion. Sacred texts for the first time in human history were scrutinized in the light of the

'higher criticism' as a result of which all religious scriptures, with the exception of the Qur'an, lost their claim to historicality. The Qur'an then stood quite alone as a historically established scripture. In this way, the intellectual revolution brought about by western civilization gave Islam a monopoly—as the only authentic representative of Religion.

5.   Then again it was this Western Civilization which, by scientifically unraveling nature's secrets, testified to the veracity of the Qur'an. Hence the credit for offering a scientific explanation of the following verse must go to western civilization.

> "We will show them our signs in the universe, and in
> their ownselves, until it becomes manifest to them that
> this is the truth (41:53).

It is thanks to the bearers of western civilization that a great number of new facts concerning the world of nature have been discovered. These facts serve to prove the authenticity of Islam on scientific bases.

For the reasons mentioned above, I am certain that western civilization cannot be regarded as a manifestation of Dajjal, as is claimed by extremists. On the contrary, in terms of its unlimited possibilities, it offers a God-sent support for Islam.

It has produced all the means and resources essential to the successful carrying out of Islamic da'wah, all over the world. This mission can be properly performed only by exploiting all the possibilities offered by modern times.

This process has already been set in motion. Today hundreds and thousands of people are accepting Islam each day, having found it to be a religion in perfect harmony with nature.

After the peace settlement at Hudaybiyya the chapter

Al-Fath was revealed in which it was said: "that it may be a sign for the believers, and that He may guide you to a straight path" (48:20).

That is to say, the symbolism of this event should prevent believers from falling a prey to the narrowness of dichotomous thinking in such matters. Rather they must strive to find a third option. This is the Hudaybiyya principle which should be adopted in our relations vis-á-vis western civilization. Only then will God's good tidings of granting a clear victory become a reality.

Da'wah Explosion

The battle of Cesmi is a significant event in the history of the Turkish caliphate. In this battle, fought in July 1770, the Ottoman naval establishment was destroyed by a Russian fleet at the harbour of Cesmi on the Aegean sea. (13/784)

A few years later, in May 1799, the British forces defeated and killed the Muslim ruler Tipu Sultan of South India. This was the beginning of the end. Subsequently, the European Christian nations conquered, directly or indirectly, all of the Muslim countries one after the other, thus establishing their own political supremacy.

Now, at this stage, the entire Muslim world reverberated with the call of jihad which was considered to be the only solution to its problems. It was felt that it was only by following this path that Muslims could regain their lost political power and glory. Therefore, the process of jihad (in the sense of militancy) was set in motion everywhere. It was a kind of explosion, the impact of which was felt all over the Muslim world. This militant jihad is still being pursued in different regions in one form or the other.

Now in the last quarter of the 20th century another revolution has occurred, but on a vaster scale. Over the last few years there has been a rapid spread of Dawah work. In any town or country, wherever you go you will witness Dawah activity. Its increase has been so great that it would not be an exaggeration to call it a Dawah explosion.

Now let us compare the dawah of the last twenty years to the jihad of 200 years. You will find a significant difference between the two so far as the result is concerned. During this prolonged and all-out war Muslims unilaterally brought down destruction upon themselves. Even after political defeat Muslims had had great resources at their disposal. But now they have lost all these in the process of continuing militancy.

On the other hand, Muslims have lost nothing in Dawah work. In fact, there have been positive gains, for every day and everywhere people are leaving their flawed, imperfectly preserved religions to enter the fold of Islam, which has been preserved in its pristine form. This is plain for all to see. A glance at the journal Al-Alamul Islami issued from Mecca, will suffice to prove this statement.

This Dawah explosion has been so sudden that it seems as though set in motion by God Himself. This is an all-encompassing movement in which both sincere as well insincere people are taking part. Even non-Muslims are playing their part in carrying this mission forward at a great speed. Both Muslims as well as non-Muslims are publishing Islamic literature on a large scale, and Islamic conferences are being held by non-Muslims as well as by Muslims. Big institutions are being established for this purpose. This is a historical process in which even anti-Islamic elements such as Salman Rushdie have also had a hand. It is because this age is marked by the spirit of enquiry. This is why, when the opponents of Islam publish a book against Islam, they inadvertently awaken the desire in millions of people to make a thorough study of the subject.

The truth is that the Dawah explosion is no simple matter. It is a historical process which started at the proper time, as predicted by the Prophet, so that with the approach of Doomsday, the message of Islam would be brought by God to every home. It seems quite obvious that this process has been set in motion according to the prediction.

First of all, propitious circumstances have been produced towards this end. For instance, modern communications; the urge to study different religions; freedom of religious expression; commercial value in religion etc. By creating such a variety of favourable conditions, God has Himself arranged for the successful outcome of Dawah work.

This is a historical process which will keep advancing on its own. It will be our great good fortune to become a conscious part of it thus securing for ourselves the blessings of Allah. While others are working for it under the pressure of historical process, we must perform this noble task by our own conscious decision.

Islam in 21st Century

Today man is in search of a new ideology. Those who can offer this new ideology to the modern man will be the leader of 21st century. F.H. Bradley has termed this new ideology as 'New Religion.' By this New Religion he actually meant unaltered version of revealed religion. But probably the concept of unaltered and altered was not known to Bradley, otherwise he would have used the term unaltered religion in place of 'New Religion.'

As a matter of fact, the search of modern man is nothing but a quest of Islam. It is a religion based on the law of nature. It is free from any sort of alteration as such it is the exponent of complete truth. Those who are not acquainted with this, call the feeling of their quest as 'New Outlook,' 'New Religion,' 'New Order,' 'New Revolution' etc. etc.

Reaching at the end of 20th century, man is confronted with a void—a void of thought. He is disillusioned with his previous ideological base. He is in search of a new and firm intellectual base to rely upon. I would like to take the case of Japan to explain my point.

Experience of Japan

Present royal family of Japan has been the ruler of Japan for the last 15 centuries. Japanese used to address their king a Kami—god. The king was supposed to have the godly attributes. But after the second world war the Japanese have come to regard their king as just a Hito—a human being. This change has been like an eruption of volcano on their intellectual level.

The Japanese had believed for 1500 years that their king, endowed with divine powers, was invincible and able to protect them from all aggressions. However, during the second world war when America devastated Hiroshima and Nagasaki by dropping two atom bombs, Japan's military power was shattered. It was the first defeat of Japan in the long span of 15 centuries. The king of Japan, Hiro Hito, announced on the radio on 15th August, 1945 that Japan had been defeated and was surrendering before the USA. This was an extremely shocking declaration for the Japanese people. Their godly king was accepting defeat. It was hard for them to believe. But the truth dawned upon them and they realized that their king too was a human being and not the incarnation of god.

This incident proved to be more devastating than the scars of atom bombs on Japan. The bombs had destroyed two of its cities temporarily but the crack in the faith eternally changed the whole inner personality of Japanese. The new generation of Japan is suffering from acute frustration. It has spiritually lost its source of confidence. The Japanese are in search of a new god today and this search is their most important issue at hand.

This state of affair, more or less, is being faced by other peoples all over the world. Everyone has lost his traditional god and everyone, consciously or unconsciously, is looking out to find a new god to substitute this void.

This is not a chance happening but a real one. It is so because religion is not an externally imposed thing. Religion is the inner urge of a human being and so imbued in his nature that it cannot be separated from his personality. Research in the field of psychology and anthropology has proved it with finality that man cannot live without god and religion. (Encyclopaedia Britannica, 1984, vol. 15, p. 628) Edmund Burke confirms the same fact when he says: "Man is by his constitution a religious animal." This is the reason why man's inner self is searching for the true and real god who can quench the thirst of his haunting soul.

Search of One God

Except for the believers in Islam, the majority of other communities have, in some or the other ways, been involved in polytheism. Zoroastrians believe in two gods. Christianity has the concept of Trinity. There are nearly 330 million gods and deities in Hinduism.

The theory of polytheism inherited by most of the communities has placed them in an awkward position of contradictions. The universe according to modern science, has complete harmony. It functions like a huge machine moving with precision and unison. The concept of one, the supreme God, therefore, is the only befitting concept for this universe. This state of affairs has made the theory of polytheism doubtful for the modern man.

The latest and decisive blow to polytheism came from what is called Superstring Theory. Prior to it, scientists conventionally believed that there were four natural forces working in the universe, that is Gravity, Electromagnetic force, Week neuclear force and Strong Neuclear force. However, keeping in view the unified system and order of the universe, the belief of four forces working behind them always urged the scientists like Einstein and others to think that this number must be brought to one. Now, a team of American scientists, after an exhaustive research, has arrived at the conclusion that there is only one force which controls the whole universe. This singular force is named Superstring. Anyone interested in further details of the Superstring theory may refer to the following books published in the US:

1. *Beyond Einstein: The Cosmic Quest for the Theory of the Universe.*

2. *Nuclear Power—Both Sides* by Jennifer Trainer and Michio Kaku.

The latest scientific revelation has brought the whole human race to the doorstep of the faith of one God or tawhid. The time has come when the idea of one God should be presented to the people of the world who would accept it as the call of their own souls and step into the fold of eternal Truth.

Result of Free Inquiry

In ancient times religion was an object of reverence and considered to be above any test or argument. But the modern scientific age has given topmost importance to inquiry and reasoning. Today people feel that any notion can be accepted only after it is tested and viewed through a free inquiry.

Modern man has applied this method to both non-religious subjects as well as religious subjects. Religious books and their teachings have ben subjected to tests of free inquiry which proved with finality that except for

Islam all other religions were not reliable. Their credibility became doubtful from the scientific and historical point of view. Let us take an example to clarify this point.

Christianity is based on the concept of Trinity. Ask any Christian theologian and he would say, "The nature of God is trinity." He interprets the Trinity as something which is, "three in one, and one in three."

Now, a modern man who wants to understand everything with reasoning, would naturally ask as to how one plus one plus one can be equal to one. The Christian theologian would first try to convince him through complex and unintelligible explanations. But when the rational mind refuses to accept them, he will simply terminate the discucssion by declaring that these are the things we cannot understand.

This ambiguity and escapism does not convince a reasoning mind. When one studies the universe objectively he finds it moulded in a mathematical frame. This is why a scientist has said that the Creator of the universe must be in possession of a highly mathematical brain. But the way the Christianity explains the attributes of this Creator is totally un-mathematical and irrational.

Again, this situation has led a major part of human community to a crossroad. The intense urge of the inner self of man commands him to find the Creator of the universe so that he may surrender himself before Him and worship Him as God. But most of the religions in vogue offer him a god which neither satisfies man's soul nor convinces his scientific and rational mind.

And thus once again we find that the modern revolution in thought and outlook has brought the contemporary human society in close proximity to Islam. The time demands that true concept of tawhid, one-ness of God, is presented before the people who will find this concept in complete harmony with the law of nature and the reasoning of science.

Contradiction in Religions

Almost everyday we come across such news that someone got frustrated with his inherited religion and embraced Islam. For example the weekly al-Dawah (Riyadh) of 17th August, 1989 has published a news item on page 41 which tells us about the acceptance of Islam by a Christian priest of Kinshasa, the capital of Zire. His name was Moya Wamoya and he was called Holy John 23. After accepting Islam this gentleman has changed his name as Usman Wamoya. When asked about the cause of renouncing Christianity, Mr Wamoya said that he was disillusioned with the factual contradictions recorded in the New Testament. For instance, these books refer to Christ as an ordinary human being at one place and as the divine son of God at the other.

When a person studies the Bible he observes an ancestoral lineage of Christ. The book of Matthew records him as the son of David. But when the reader approaches the book of Mark, Christ becomes Son of God. Thus the same personality has different identities. He is son of a man at one stage and Son of God at the other.

The Bible is full of such discrepancies which compel its reader to think that if it is the book of God, it must have been subjected to human interference and alterations. Probably the present Bible is a drastically changed version of its original form. There is no question of so much and so obvious contradictions existing in a divine Book.

The case of the Bible has adversely affected the psyche of modern man. He has become indifferent towards all religious books. Nevertheless, his soul and nature craves for religion. Religion is the only solace for man's inner self and his external life. He is disgusted and rebellious towards interpolated religions. But his whole existence is crying for the true and unadulterated religion of God. At this juncture, if he is exposed to Islam he will accept it as avidly as someone dying of thirst will accept a jug of water.

Failure of Materialistic Religion

As stated earlier, the notion of treating religion as a sanctified subject does not exist anymore. Today it is as exposed to enquiry and evaluation as any other subject. For unbiased study and analysis of religion, certain new approaches have come into effect such as Higher Criticism, Textual Criticism, Historical Criticism etc. This investigative attitude applied to religion led to the studies which revealed the fact that no religion, except Islam, is reliable in its present form.

Subsequently a new 'religion' emerged in the guise of materialism. Its philosophy was that every thing that really exists is material in nature. This breeded the outlook of achieving maximum materialistic gains in practical life. It propagated the theory that materialistic acquisitions were the only source of man's happiness.

But this ideology failed both at the level of thought and practice. At the level of thought this failure is reflected in the limitations of science. Extensive researches and studies were carried out in various fields of science with the hope of discovering the ultimate realities. But these proved to be hopeless endeavours. The instrumentalities of science were miserably ineffective and inadequate to unveil the ultimate reality of existence. Sir James Jeans endorses this view in the following words:

> *Physical science sets out to study a world of matter and radiation and finds that it cannot describe or picture the nature of either, even to itself. Photons, electrons and protons have been found as meaningless to the physicist as x, y, z are to a child on its first day of learning algebra. The most we hope for at the moment is to discover ways of manipulating x, y, z without knowing what they are.* (Sir James Jeans, The New Background of Science)

The advancements in science have only intensified our realization of ignorance. The more we know, the more we are aware of our ignorance. Einstein terms this situation as "extracting an incomprehensible from another incomprehensible."

Similar failure of materialism has also been experienced in practical life. Today's world provided man opportunities to earn more and more, which he exploited to the maximum. But the huge accumulation of wealth and means of comfort ultimately filled his life with nothing but boredom. In spite of all materialistic resources, man could not find real peace and satisfaction.

When scientific and technological advancements made all the luxuries of the world within easy reach of man, he thought there was no need of any paradise in the life hereafter. He forgot that his ambitions of this life could not escape the inevitability of limitations and disavantages. Amidst the glittering heap of wealth, the happiness remained a mirage for him.

A glimpse of this tragedy of the modern age can be had from Vance Packer's 358-page book, *The Ultra Rich* published from New York in 1989. The book contains real life portrayals of thirty super rich Americans, each one worth 425 million dollars or more. The author interviewed them personally and observed that all of them, without exception, were suffering from discontentment. Their palatial mansions have so vast lawns that a 707 Boeing plane can easily land there. But all this material abundance is like "a verdant cage" according to one of these ultra rich people. Another one feels disgusted of his wealth and says "I don't know what the hell to do with it!"

Such experiences of "materialistic religion" have made the modern man doubtful towards materialism. This 'new religion' could neither respond to his intellectual queries nor provide peace and contentment which he instinctively desires in practical life. Like interpolated religions, the materialistic religion has also disappointed him. He deserves and needs to be guided to the reassuring solace of the true religion of God.

Religion of Brotherhood and Equality

Discrimination of inequality between man and man is continuing since time immemorial. In the past, it was due to influence of superstition. People had various superstitious beliefs which justified the theory of inequality and division. They believed that white races were created with superior elements, while the blacks with inferior ones. Hence the notion of superior and inferior races was considered natural and justified.

The modern age has, however, proved this concept to be totally baseless. Inquiry and analysis of facts revealed that beliefs of racial inequality were imaginary and mythical. Several books have been written on the subject with scientific reasonings. *The Race Question in Modern Science,* by J. Comas (1956) is one of the important books in this regard.

At present man finds himself standing on a bisecting road. On one side he faces his inherited conventional religion which still preaches inequality among humanity. On the other side he finds his scientific knowledge which rejects the theory of racial discrimination as sheer absurdity. The modern man realizes that he cannot shape his life on scientific basis if he continues to believe in his inherited religion.

Islam is the only solution to this problem. Being a religion free from any adulteration, its teachings are most accurate, authentic and perfect. Islamic principles and thoughts are not only in harmony with scientific facts but it is the only religion that carries a brilliant tradition of equality and brotherhood among all human beings. H.G. Wells has accepted that Islam did not merely preach justice and equality but implemented it in practical life in an exceptional manner. He has explained it in the following words:

> They (Muslims) created a society more free from widespread cruelty and social oppression than any society had ever been in the world before. (H.G. Wells, The Outline of History, p. 325)

Well known Hindu reformer Swami Vivekananda has acknowledged the practice of equality and indiscrimination in Islam in the following words:

> My experience is that if ever any religion approached to this equality in an appreciable manner, it is Islam and Islam alone. (Swami Vivekananda, Letters of Vivekanananda, p. 379)

This practical side of Islam has made this religion an exclusive bearer of truth and justice. Throughout the annals of known world history, one finds Islam as the only religion that can help in building a society based on the practised principles of brotherhood, equality and justice. The Declaration of Human Rights" of the UNO, in its present form, is a mere utopia of words. There is no precedent of practicality behind this flowery declaration. The teachings of Islam, one the other hand, have the well-known exemplary tradition as to how the ideals can actually be realized in real life.

These are but a few from among the numerous aspects which I have attempted to present before you to show the opportunities for the call and invitation to Islam. The revolutionary changes in the thought and outlook of contemporary society have brought man very close to Islam. Like the instinctive pursuit of some upright persons called Hunafa of the era of ignorance before Islam, the whole of humanity has become a compulsive seeker of Islam today.

This situation has opened up the doors of tremendous new opportunities for da'wah—call and invitation to Islam. If these opportunities are availed properly, there is no doubt that the 21st century would be the century of Islam.

Passion for Da'wah

I wish to conclude by mentioning an interesting incident which serves as a booster for da'wah activities. It concerns physicist Murray Gell-Mann of the US who won Physics Nobel Prize in 1969. He was acknowledged for his contribution in bringing order to man's knowledge of the seemingly chaotic profusion of subatomic particles.

When Mr Gell-Mann made his prize-winning discovery in the field of physics, he was overcome with the irresistible desire to make others aware of its facts. He innovated a scheme for this purpose. In the American city of Auspen he arranged a cabaret show and invited the educated people. The show started and gradually reached its peak. Then suddenly some strange thing happened. In the words of the reporter, "Near the end of the show, physicist Murray Gell-Mann jumped up from the audience, dashed to the stage and exclaimed, "Stop everything! I have to explain to you the theory of the Universe. I understood how everything works."

After the discovery of a truth, one cannot help but announce it to the world. Like a bursting force it must come out of his existence and deluge the surroundings. Discovery makes a man da'i—the caller of Truth. The case of Islamic da'wah is the same. If we could truly and sincerely realize the fact that tremendous opportunities are lying around us for spreading the message of Islam in the world, our body and soul would become restless to let this message be out. With even sharper intensity, we would behave like Murray Gell-Mann. We would dash before the people and proclaim, "stop everything and listen! We have the most important, the most momentous message for you. You accutely need it. Your life in this world and the life hereafter will be dismal without knowing this reality, and the reality is Islam, the true religion of soul."

Ambassadors of Islam

Umm Haram bint Milhan, a Sahabiya, (a companion of the Prophet) was married to Ubadah ibn as-Samit Ansari. Along with her husband she undertook several trips to foreign countries. Now her grave is in Cyprus, and is called the grave of the pious woman (*Hayat As-Sahaba* 1/592). The grave of Khalid ibn al-Walid, who was born in Mecca, is in Hims (Syria).

The same is the case with the majority of the Companions of the Prophet. At the time of the Prophet's demise, his companions numbered more than one lakh. However it is worth noting that if you go to Mecca and Medina you will find only a small number of graves there. The reason for this is that these companions left Arabia and spread to various countries far and beyond its borders. The majority of them breathed their last in various Asian and African countries, where their graves still exist.

Why did this happen? It was because during his last days the Prophet gathered his companions together in the mosque in Medina and addressed them in these words: God has sent me as His messenger for the entire world. So you do not differ with one another. And spread in the land and communicate my message to people inhabiting other places besides Arabia. (Seerat Ibn Hisham 4/279).

It was this injunction of the Prophet that led to the Sahaba (companions of the Prophet) settling in foreign lands. In those countries they either did business or earned their living by hard work, all the while communicating to their non-Muslim compatriots the message of monotheism which they had received from the Prophet. Every one of them thus became a virtual ambassador of Islam. This resulted in Islam spreading across the globe. Its evidence can still be seen in the inhabited world of that time.

I feel history is repeating itself in modern times. New circumstances, produced in the wake of industrial revolution, have resulted in Muslims leaving their homelands to spread all over the world. Today, whichever part of the globe you visit, you will find Muslims there. Mosques and Islamic institutions have come up everywhere. Muslims have settled in these countries either for work or for business. However, in respect of their religion, their actual position is that of Islam's representatives. It is as if each one of them is an ambassador of God. Now the need of the hour is to awaken the missionary spirit in these Muslims settled in foreign lands, so that they may effectively communicate the message of Islam—a task of universal magnitude made incumbent upon them by their new sets of circumstances.

PART VII

Asian Muslims And
Modern Challenges

Asian Muslims have been faced with problems on diverse fronts for more than a hundred years and have been struggling to meet the challenges since the second half of the 19th century. The Muslim leaders of those times were of the view that the actual cause of all their problems was the political domination of the western nations, and that their problems could be solved only by bringing to an end that political domination.

This goal was fully achieved after the second world war, when all Muslim countries became free from foreign rule. However, their problems, far from being solved have persisted till today with undiminished intensity.

What is the reason for this? The reason is traceable to the fact that western dominance was, in fact, the result of modern industrial civilization. Since the western nations continued to grow as industrial powers, even after losing their political power, their domination continued, the only difference being that where their domination had earlier been a direct one, it now became indirect.

Given the negative results of their struggles, certain Muslim intellectuals have attributed their failure to solve their problems to their industrial backwardness. They hold that only by the acquisition of industrial power similar to that of the developed nations can their destiny be changed.

This, however, is not the solution to our problems. Time does not standstill. New developments are constantly taking place. This means that, even if, by a supreme effort, we managed to enter the industrial age, by the time we did so, the western nations, in the words of Elvin Toffler, would have entered the 'super industrial age.' In this way we would continue to lag behind, and our actual problems would continue to remain unsolved.

The kind of problems and challenges Muslims are faced with today, at political, economic and cultural levels, is in no way a new state of affairs never before encountered.

In their long history the Muslims have repeatedly experienced such situations in various forms. History, shows, moreover, that the Muslim Ummah has always emerged far more powerful and consolidated after passing through the dangers and challenges of the various phases of their history.

Now, what we must grasp is how such problems and challenges were formerly faced by the Ummah. The sole answer offered by history is that on each occasion of adversity success was achieved through the da'wah power of Islam.

The Mongols, barbarous and bloody in their methods of warfare, succeeded in inflicting extraordinary harm on Muslims in the middle of the thirteenth century. They appeared invincible. But then, miraculously, the daw'ah power of Islam emerged and the Mongols were conquered. Referring to this event, an orientalist observes: 'The religion of the Muslims had conquered where their arms had failed.'

Muslims must rise today with the help of this da'wah power of Islam. If they were to perform their da'wah work properly, their condition would certainly change for the better. They would themselves benefit as has been expressed in the Qur'an in these words: Good and evil deeds are not alike. Requite evil with good, and he, between whom and you is enmity, will become your dearest friend (4:34).

The opportunities to revive this da'wah process of Islam have increased to an extraordinary degree. The scientific study of religions has proved that all other religions besides Islam have lost their credibility. No other religion is historically credible. Whereas in every scientific analysis Islam has proved to be authentic. In this way Islam is in a position to gain an unopposed victory.

So far as human 'isms' are concerned, they have all been failures, the most obvious example being the collapse of the communist empire. While it was still in existence, the world was under the misapprehension that it possessed an idealogy. But this false conviction gave way when the communist empire fell apart in 1991. Now, all over the world there is an idealogical vacuum. And it is the kind of vacuum which can be filled only by Islam. Now the time has finally come for Muslims to rise with the power of Islamic da'wah to build a new history for Islam through an idealogical conquest of the nations.

What we have to do now is repeat that experience of our history which has unfailingly proved its success at all times. That is, we must avail of the da'wah power of Islam in order to counter the challenges and problems we are faced with. In their long history Muslims have always gained success through da'wah power and today, too, by putting it to good use, they can certainly emerge victorious.

The secret of da'wah power conquering all in its path

lies in its emphasis on profitability. God's law for this world is that what is useful for people gains stability and acceptability among the people. Islam, of all religions, is the most beneficial. It provides the answer to man's search for truth. It furnishes man with a true idealogy of life. It gives man mental peace. It is exactly in accordance with human nature. It helps man discover the thoroughfare by which he can safely complete his journey from this world to the hereafter. Undoubtedly there is nothing more profitable to man, and that is what makes Islam the most acceptable of religions. The partial success of da'wah work can be seen even today, even when it is not being performed in an organized way at the community level.

Over the last one hundred years countless political sacrifices have been made, without there having been any real gain, whereas during the same period tens of thousands of people, impressed by the teachings of Islam, have entered the fold of Islam.

Islam is a religion of nature. It has the only uninterpolated scriptures. It is such factors as these which have made Islam into an effective force on its own. That is why people continue to embrace Islam in every country and in every region of the world. You may not be able to carry out elaborate research on the subject, but if you just read through the weekly Al'Daw'ah, published in Riyadh, you will find such instances in almost every one of its issues.

The importance of daw'ah has been established in both theory and practice. The need of the hour is, therefore, the adoption of daw'ah work as our most important programme, and the diversion of all our strength and resources towards this end.

This paper was presented at the Conference on 'Muslims in Asia at Colombo, Sri Lanka on August 26, 1993

Importance of Education

The field of education, covering ethics, religion, skills and general knowledge, is a very broad and very vital one. The importance of learning in enabling the individual to put his potentials to optimal use is self-evident. Without education, the training of the human minds is incomplete. No individual is a human being in the proper sense until he has been educated.

Education makes man a right thinker and a correct decision-maker. It achieves this by bringing him knowledge from the external world, teaching him to reason, and acquainting him with past history, so that he may be a better judge of the present. Without education, man, as it were, is shut up in a windowless room. With education, he finds himself in a room with all its windows open to the outside world.

This is why Islam attaches such great importance to knowledge and education. The Qur'an, it should be noted repeatedly asks us to observe the earth and heavens. This instils in man the desire to learn natural science. When the Qur'an began to be revealed, the first word of its first verse was 'Iqra!' that is, 'Read.' Education is thus the starting point of every successful human activity.

All the books of hadith have a chapter on knowledge (ilm). In Sahih Bukhari, there is a chapter entitled, "The virtue of one who acquires ilm (learning) and imparts it to others." In the hadith, the scholar is accorded great respect. According to one tradition, the ink of a scholar's pen is more precious than the blood of a martyr, the reason being that while a martyr is engaged in the task of defence, an alim (scholar) builds individuals and nations along positive lines. In this way, he bestows upon the world a real life treasure.

The very great importance attached to learning in Islam is illustrated by an event in the life of the Prophet. At the battle of Badr, in which the Prophet was victorious, seventy of his enemies were taken prisoner. Now these captives were all literate people. So, in order to benefit from their erudition, the Prophet declared that if each prisoner taught ten Medinan children how to read and write, that would serve as his ransom and he would be set free. This was the first school in the history of Islam, established by the Prophet himself. It was of no matter to him that all its teachers were non-Muslims, all were prisoners of war, and all were likely to create problems again for Islam and Muslims once they were released. This Sunnah of the Prophet showed that whatever the risk involved, education was paramount.

Islam not only stresses the importance of learning, but demonstrates how all the factors necessary to progress in learning have been provided by God. An especially vital factor is the freedom to conduct research. Such freedom was encouraged right from the beginning, as is illustrated by an incident which took place after the Prophet had migrated from Mecca to Medina. There he saw some people atop the date palms pollinating them. Since dates were not grown in Mecca the Prophet had to ask what these people were doing to the trees. He threreupon forbade them to do this, and the following year date crop was very poor as compared to previous year. When the Prophet asked the reason, he was told that the yield depended on pollination. He then told the date-growers to resume this practice, admitting that they knew more about "worldly matters" than he did.

In this way, the Prophet separated practical matters from religion, thus paving the way for the free conduct of research throughout the world of nature and the adoption of conclusions based thereon. This great emphasis placed on exact knowledge resulted in the awakening of a great desire for learning among the Muslims of the first phase. This process began in Mecca, then reached Medina and Damascus, later centering on Baghdad. Ultimately it entered Spain. Spain flourished, with extraordinary progress made in various academic and scientific disciplines. This flood of scientific progress then entered Europe, ultimately ushering in the modern, scientific age.

Religion and Politics

With the independence of India in 1947, two countries India and Pakistan—came into existence on the subcontinent. In both these countries there was a secular group and a religious group. The secular group held that the system of the country's governance should be run along purely secular lines, independently of religion, whereas the thinking of the religious group was quite the contrary. They insisted that the political system of the country should be governed in accordance with the dictates of religion.

This religion-based system was called Nizam-e-Mustafa in Pakistan, and Ram Rajya in India. Although in both of these countries political power fell into the hands of the secular group, in neither country did the religious group remain silent. Rather, they pursued the path of confrontation in order to attain their goal of establishing the system of government on the basis of religion. To put it another way, they opted for the path of force in order to replace the secular system with the system of government of their choice.

ISLAM AND PEACE

This struggle culminated in Pakistan in April 1979 with Bhutto's execution, which was termed judicial murder by Bhutto himself. Pakistan's religious class felt that Bhutto's existence presented the greatest obstacle to introducing Nizam-e-Mustafa. He had, therefore, to be eliminated. But the experiment revealed that Nizam-e-Mustafa could not find a place in the life of the nation even after the removal of Bhutto. The hold of the secular group persisted.

The Ram Rajya movement in India culminated in December 1992 with the demolition of the Babari Masjid at Ayodhya. Even after a period of two years, subsequent to the demolition, the Ram Rajya movement has not been able to move even one step ahead. The secular group continues to dominate the political arena.

Whether it be right or wrong, from the ideological point of view, to subordinate politics to religion, the experiment of the last fifty years tells us that our present *course* is certainly not the right one. It would be more true to say that the present course, in terms of non-achievement of goals, has been counter-productive. What has come into being, and what is going to be achieved in the effort to consolidate the position of religion is in no way a religious system, but is rather a course of destruction. This destructive element has only added to the general ruination of the country.

How did all these efforts on our part backfire? It can be traced quite simply to our violation of realities. Innumerable natural causes have to cooperate in this world in order to bring about a significant event. Someone has said very pertinently: 'Politics is the art of the possible.' That is, only when conducive factors are present is a leader able to realise a political event. It is not possible even for the greatest of leaders to bring about a political revolution simply by dint of his own efforts without the cooperation of external elements.

The Islamization of Pakistan and the Hinduization of India simply failed to take shape; despite a 50-year bloody struggle neither could Pakistan be Islamized nor India Hinduized.

As a result of the intellectual development of the last several hundred years, the world mindset is now entirely against a state based on religion. This world-wide intellectual revolution is known as secularism. While religion is founded on *faith*, secularism is based on *reason*. The majority of the educated classes in modern times has accepted that matters of state should be kept independent of sacred scriptures, and that they should be dealt with on the basis of *reason*. That is to say that world opinion is in favour of the secular rather than the religious state.

India presents no exception to this rule. As a result of the modernization of education over the last two hundred years, the new Indian generation thinks along the same lines as the rest of the world. Like all other countries, India too is a part of the global village.

Given this reality, if a state based on religion had to be established, a sea change in world thinking—on a purely ideological plane—should have to be effected. Without a universal, intellectual revolution, it would be impossible to found a religious state in the manner of a political island even at the level of one's own country.

The only practicable course to follow in this matter is to acknowledge the reality. Besides this, there is almost no other choice. Now the time has come for a true patriot ultimately to change himself in the interests of his country. Accepting his limitations, he should mould himself in accordance with the reality rather than waste time in pursuing the unattainable goal of a reality moulded to suit his own purposes.

Having given due consideration to all aspects of this issue, I have come to the conclusion that without going into the ideological discussion of what is right and what is wrong, all the concerned parties should come to agree in this matter on a practicable formula in the wider interests of the country.

What is most important in this connection is to set the election process in motion without any hindrance. Elections should be free and fair. Whichever group is subsequently elected to power should be given full freedom to complete its term.

During this period, the defeated group should never launch a campaign to oust the victor group. It should, on the contrary, direct its efforts to impressing its ideology upon the public which is later to vote it to power. The five-year period should be devoted to bringing about changes in public opinion by peaceful methods. If the defeated group succeeds in influencing the voters, it will automatically be voted to power in the next elections. It will then find the opportunity to reconstruct the country's political and administrative systems along its own ideological lines.

Wholehearted acceptance of election results, followed by the adoption of a waiting policy, while one's own ideology continues to be propagated in a peaceful manner, is the only practicable course. This is the only way to influence the minds of the voters, without running counter to the genuine interests of the country.

Islam in India

A good number of Muslim leaders seems to be keen to promote Islam and Islamic values in India by trying to project the view that Islam needs their protection. Nothing could be farther from the truth. They would do well to cast even a cursory look at India's history to realise that their approach is doing more harm than any good to the cause of Islam or Muslims in India.

The founder of the Moghul empire in India, Zahiruddin Mohammad Babar (1483-1530 AD), first invaded the subcontinent in 1519. After several battles, he finally captured Delhi and Agra in 1526 to establish the Moghul rule. He was succeeded by his son, Nasiruddin Humayun.

Jalaluddin Mohammad Akbar (1542-1605), son of Humayun, ascended the Moghul throne in 1556 after his father's death. At that time Moghul rule was marked by instability. One reason was that Moghuls, being foreign invaders, aroused great resentment among the local people. To end this state of unrest, Akbar resorted to his policy of Sulh-e-Kul (peace with all concerned) and Din-e-Ilah. The religion Akbar proposed was not, in fact, a religion. It was rather a piece of strategy designed to put an end to hatred that had developed between the Muslims and the non-Muslims during the reigns of earlier Sultans of Delhi. In spite of its apparent clumsiness, the strategy worked and Akbar by securing the cooperation of the majority of people, and despite the opposition of the orthodox section of his courtiers, succeeded in bringing about political stability in the country and people prospered. Indeed, from the reign of Akbar to that of Shahjehan, tens of thousands of people voluntarily accepted Islam and entered its egalitarian fold. The key factor in creating this propitious atmosphere was the policy followed by Akbar.

We know nothing of Akbar's intentions. But even if he had been as evil as some people thought him to be, the above analysis retains its validity. It is an irrefutable fact that Akbar's policy of appeasement resulted in the rapid spread of Islam along with an atmosphere of peace and tranquillity. Even if, as a man, he was ill-intentioned, the results he achieved as a monarch will bear out the words of the Prophet: There is no doubt that God will help this religion "even if it be through a sinner".

In contrast, during the reign of the last Moghul emperor, Mohiuddin Aurangzeb (who assumed the title of Alamgir, the world conqueror), relations between Muslim and non-Muslims once again turned sour, for his policies antagonised all communities and castes: Marathas, Rajputs, Sikhs, Hindus and even intelligent Muslims began to dislike him and his policies. As a natural consequence, society again became tension-ridden. The process of dissemination of Quran's teachings which was well under way as a result of Akbar's policies was halted. Hindu-Muslim antagonism thus put an end to the friction-free atmosphere which is a must for the spread of Islam.

After Aurangzeb, the Moghul empire went into a decline. At that point, however, the situation was saved by the appearance of Sufis on the scene. The Sufis set about establishing khanqah (monasteries) all over the country and revived the traditions of earlier Sufi saints to spread the message of love, elimination of hatred between man and man and to emphasise the oneness of mankind and that of God, the Almighty. They met with extraordinary success. Their following increased both among the Hindus and Muslims until they became the most influential element of society in shaping the character of the people.

Just as the hatred engendered by earlier Sultans and Babar was nullified by Akbar, the hatred aroused by Aurangzeb was extinguished by the Sufis. It was then that there came into existence an atmosphere truly conducive to the communication of the message of Islam. That is why, in spite of the Moghul empire's decline and fall after Aurangzeb the spread of Islam was actually accelerated. That the spread of Islam also cemented the foundation of the nation became evident during the socalled Mutiny of 1857 when Hindus and Muslims, Peshwas and molavis, women of valour like Rani of Jhansi and Begum Hazrat Mahal, fought shoulder to shoulder to regain the nation's pride and independence from the alien English.

This process of spreading of Islam continued until Mr Mohammad Ali Jinnah (1876-1948) appeared on the scene. It was he who invented, under western inspiration, the 'two-nation theory,' thereby creating afresh a chasm between Hindus and Muslims and an atmosphere of constant friction between them by getting the country divided with the blessings of aliens who realised that they could not no longer stay and rule over us all. If this theory of separateness had remained in the realm of ideology alone, relatively little harm would have ensued. Unfortunately, he and his ilk chose to stress the geographical aspect of this divisive concept. As a result, we are left with holding the baby of this hatred-filled concept in the form of a permanent confrontation and friction between the two major sections of Indian people in the form of a political principle which more often than not brought to the fore by politicians of all hues and colour.

The 'two-nation theory' was, in effect, an off-shoot of the constant friction and confrontation stirred up between the two peoples and it was under exceptional circumstnaces that this concept gained popularity among the Muslims. Indeed, the whole country responded to the 'two-nation theory'. The greatest religion for both communities became Hindu-Muslim hatred. This poisonous form of politics saw its culmination in 1947 when a wall of hatred—a wall far stronger than the Berlin Wall—rose between the two communities.

By the middle of the twentieth century, the dissemination of Islam in this country had come to a hal once again. The principal reason for this interrruption was Mr Jinnah's brand of politics spewing bitterness and hatred all over again. and once again the heavens await the day when this atmosphere of enmity and abhorrence for each other among the Muslims and others will dissipate and dissolve and the door for acceptance of Islam as a religion of peace, tranquillity and prosperity will open once again as before.

Islam is a natural faith, free of all adulterations. By sheer virtue of its own strength, it can make inroads into the hearts of the people. The only barrier to its natural acceptance by others is the atmosphere of belligerence.

If the message of Islam is to be successfully communicated, Muslims themselves must prevent any unfavourable atmosphere from coming in its way. If Muslims can achieve only this, Islam will begin again to command respect from others and enter the hearts of people on its own. There will be no further need to make any direct efforts towards this end.

PART VIII

Islam: An Ideological Movement for a Peaceful Co-existence

Irfan A. Omar interviewed Maulana Wahiduddin Khan, President The Islamic Centre, New Delhi and Editor-in-Chief *Al-Risala* magazine, during his visit to washington in February 1998.

Q. How do you find the general situation of the Muslim community here and their reaction to your talks?

A. I am very hopeful of the Muslim community here. Mainly because I do not measure people and their situations with ideals. In my view, there are no ideals. When you are looking for ideals then there is always disappointment. I always measure situations with practical possibilities.

We know that now the number of Muslims is increasing all over the world. People are converting on their own. I see a divine plan in it. After the Prophet (PBUH) the word of Islam spread throughout the world, people went out as traders and took with them the message of Islam. Similarly, Muslim and non-Muslim interaction today is making it possible again for the former to present Islam to the latter on an unprecedented scale.

I commented while talking to some resident Muslims here over the fact that they left their countries in search of economic opportunities and many of them have found such opportunities and prospered here (in the United States and the Western world in general). Now all they have to do is to turn their intentions for the sake of Islam; continue to strive in whatever they do in making an honest living, just intend to do it for the cause of Islam and there they will find themselves spreading Islam in all kinds of situations.

My feeling is that there is a *dawa* explosion everywhere nowadays. Everywhere there is talk of Islam. For example, someone mentioned that he went into a bookstore in Chicago and asked the salesperson about the number of copies that were sold of the Satanic Verses. The answer was "three." Then he asked, "how many copies of the Qur'an translation were sold today?" The answer was, "seventy." So in my view, even Salman Rushdie is helping in the cause/propagation of Islam. By selling three copies of his own book, he helped create interest in the Qur'an which far outweighed the interest in his own book; a ratio of 3.70. So, there is an explosion of *dawa* and people are writing, publishing, talking and debating about Islam everywhere, not only in the US but everywhere in the world.

At the same time there is a shift in the style of thinking of many people from violent activism to peaceful activism. This is a refreshing change from my last visit. Now more and more people are convinced of peaceful means for the defense of Islam and Muslims. I have strongly urged that violence is against the spirit of the age and it must be discarded. Peaceful activism is the Islamic way of activism and it should be utilized. So during this visit, I have noticed that people are beginning to realize this factor and in this I see that history is moving in the right direction for the cause of Islam.

Q. Do you think that the American culture or Western culture in general is conducive for the growth of Islam?

A. Absolutely. I was talking to someone during a recent conference on *Dajjal* and I mentioned that those who call Western culture a manifestation of *Dajjal* should know that we need many more of such *Dajjals*. You see, for first time in recent history Western culture has caused great awakening. For the first time religious freedom was granted and religious persecution condemned. It is Western culture that invented modern means of communication. It is Western culture that accomplished major achievements in science and technology and therefore helped discover the ayat (signs) of Allah hidden in nature. Books like Maurice Bucaille's *The Bible, the Quran and Science* became possible only after Western culture had unfolded the proofs of God in nature and in science.

But today Muslims are stuck in those aspects of Western culture that are demeaning, antithetical to Islam. They should, instead, focus upon those aspects of the West that are productive, intellectual, constructive, moral and so on.

Q. Many Muslims tend to see non-Muslims as 'the other' as it were, to the extent that there appears a clear dichotomy between Muslims and non-Muslims, us and them, good and evil. Does this attitude have any basis in Islam?

A. The Quran and Hadith are opposed to this attitude of creating the "other" and constructing divisions between 'us' and 'them'. The Quran says, "Call (people) to the Way of your Lord with wisdom and with beautiful preaching and argue with them in ways that are best (16:125); Repel (evil) with goodness. Then he who hated you will become your friend (41:34)."

So revolutionary is this idea, that even an enemy is to be treated as a friend. One should consider even one's enemy as a potential friend and respond to his mistreatment with goodness. Therefore, according to the Quran, we do not have the right to call anyone kafir which is the situation that emerges when the Muslims see non-Muslims as the 'other.' To call people kafir just because they do not claim to be Muslim is to violate God's injunctions. *Kafir* literally means *munkir* as translated by Shah Abdul Qadir, *Munkir* is someone who rejects or conceals the truth. If the message has never been presented to a people then they cannot be called *munkir* let alone *kafir*. Therefore, all races and peoples of the world should be viewed as human beings who are potential allies; allies of Muslims against unbelief. And they should be presented with the theory as well as practice of Islam.

All the prophets who came in this world with a message called out, "O people," "O brothers," "O my community;" none of them said, "O *kafirun*." Therefore, we should learn from this prophetic style as to how to communicate God's message in this world. If *dawa* is not done with its etiquettes which means that in spite of hate and persecution we do not react or curse those whom we intend to invite to the message, then there is little chance that anyone will listen to us and respect us.

Until we have exhausted the arguments and have presented the entire message to those who do not have it, we have no right to put the blame upon them. I would go so far as to say that even then we do not have the right to call non-Muslims *kafir*.

In the Qur'an, God declared the Makkan *munkirin* as

kafirs. It is God who called them as such but it is not right for humans to judge people by such labels since only God knows who is a *munkir* and who is not. So, our job as Muslims is to keep the work of *dawa* and leave it to Allah to see whether they are *kafir* or not.

In short, whether Western people or any other people do not see Islam as truth we do not have the right to call them *kafir*. In essence, we cannot perceive them as the "other;" it is not permissible for us to view them as such.

Q. What is the situation of Muslims in India? We hear of continuing disturbances between Muslims and Hindus as well as about the violent clashes which come would perceive as the persecution of Muslims at the hands of Hindus and Indian government. How do you respond to that?

A. The situation of Indian Muslims today is better than Muslims in any other place in the world. The reason I say this is because nowhere is there as great a number of Muslims as in India. Until a few years ago, Indonesia was regarded as constituting the largest Muslim population. But now that situation has been reversed; there are more Muslims in India than anywhere else.

Secondly, Muslims in India have far better opportunities than many other places. For any type of development and progress, both material and social, two things are required; peace and freedom. Both are available in India compared to many Muslim countries. In Pakistan there is freedom but no peace; in some Arab countries there is relative peace but little freedom. India is one country where both are present.

Non-Violence and Islam

Non-violence should never be confused with inaction or passivity. Non-violence is action in the full sense of the word. Rather it is more forceful an action than that of violence. It is a fact that non-violent activism is more powerful and effective than violent activism.

Non-violent activism is not limited in its sphere. It is a course of action which may be followed in all matters.

Whenever individuals, groups or communities are faced with a problem, one way to solve it is by resorting to violence. The better way is to attempt to solve the problem by peaceful means, avoiding violence and confrontation. Peaceful means may take various forms. In fact, it is the nature of the problem which will determine which of these peaceful methods is applicable to the given situation.

Islam is a religion which teaches non-violence. According to the Qur'an, God does not love *fasad*, violence. What is meant here by *fasad* is clearly expressed in verse 205 of the second *surah*. Basically, *fasad* is that action which results in disruption of the social system, causing huge losses in terms of lives and property.

Conversely, we can say with certainty that God loves non-violence. He abhors violent activity being indulged in human society, as a result of which people have to pay the price with their possessions and lives. This is supported by other statements in the Qur'an. For instance, we are told in the Qur'an that peace is one of God's names (59:23). Those who seek to please God are assured by verse 5 of the sixteenth *surah* that they will be guided by Him to "the paths of peace." Paradise, which is the final destination of the society of God's choice, is referred to in the Qur'an as "the home of peace" (89:30), etc.

The entire spirit of the Qur'an is in consonance with this concept. For instance, the Qur'an attaches great importance to patience. In fact, patience is set above all other Islamic virtues with the exceptional promise of reward beyond measure. (39:10)

Patience implies a peaceful response or reaction, whereas impatience implies a violent response. The word *sabr* exactly expresses the notion of non-violence as it is understood in modern times. That patient action is non-violent action as has been clearly expressed in the Qur'an. According to one tradition, the Prophet of Islam observed: God grants to *rifq* (gentleness) what he does not grant to *unf* (violence). (*Sunan*, Abu Dawood, 4/255)

The word *rifq* has been used in this hadith as an antithesis to *unf*. These terms convey exactly what is meant by violence and non-violence in present times. This hadith clearly indicates the superiority of the non-violent method.

God grants on non-violence what He does not grant to violence is no simple matter. It has very wide and deep implications. It embodies an eternal law of nature. By the very law of nature all bad things are associated with violence, while all good things are associated with non-violence.

Violent activities breed hatred in society, while non-violent activities elicit love. Violence is the way of destruction while non-violence is the way of construction. In an atmosphere of violence, it is enmity which flourishes, while in an atmosphere of non-violence, it is friendship which flourishes. The method of violence gives way to negative values while the method of non-violence is marked by positive values. The method of violence embroils people in problems, while the method of non-violence leads people to the exploiting of opportunities. In short, violence is death, non-violence is life.

Both the Qur'an and the hadith have attached great importance to *jihad*. What is *jihad*? *Jihad* means struggle, to struggle one's utmost. It must be appreciated at the outset that this word is used for non-violent struggle as opposed to violent struggle. One clear proof of this is the verse of the Qur'an (25:52) which says: Perform *jihad* with this (i.e. the word of the Qur'an) most strenuously.

The Qur'an is not a sword or a gun. It is a book of ideology. In such a case performing *jihad* with the Qur'an would mean an ideological struggle to conquer peoples' hearts and minds through Islam's superior philosophy.

In the light of this verse of the Qur'an, *jihad* in actual fact is another name for peaceful activism or non-violent activism. Where *qital* is violent activism, *jihad* is non-violent activism.

Peaceful Beginning

When the Qur'an began to be revealed, the first verse of the revelation conveyed the injunction: 'Read!' (*Iqra*) (96:1). By perusing this verse we learn about the initiation

of Islamic action. It begins from the point where there is
hope of continuing the movement along peaceful lines,
and not from that point where there are chances of its
being marred by violence.

When the command of 'Iqra' was revealed, there were
many options available in Mecca as starting points for a
movement. For instance, one possible starting point was
to launch a movement to purify the Kabah of the 360 idols
installed in it. But, by pursuing such a course, in such a
case the Islamic movement would certainly have had to
face a violent reaction from the Quraysh. An alternative
starting point could have been an attempt to secure a seat
in the Dar-al-Nadwa (Mecca's parliament). At that time
almost the whole of Arabia was under the direct or
indirect influence of the Roman and Sasanid empires. If
the freeing of Arabia from this influence had been made
the starting point, this would also have been met with an
immediate violent reaction on the part of the Quraysh.

Leaving aside these options, the path followed was
that of reading the Qur'an, an activity that could be with
certainty continued along peaceful lines: no violent reaction
would ensue from engaging in such an activity.

The Prophet of Islam followed this principle throughout
his life. His policy was that of adopting non-violent
methods in preference to violent methods. It is this policy
which was referred to by Aishah, the Prophet's wife, in
these words: Whenever the Prophet had to opt for one of
two ways, he almost always opted for the easier one.
(Fathul Bari 6/654)

What are the advantages of non-violent activism over
violent activism? They are briefly stated as under:

1. According to the Qur'an there are two faculties in
every human being which are mutually antipathetic. One

is the ego, and the other is the conscience called respectively *nafs ammara* and *nafs lawwama.* (The Qur'an, 12:53; 75:26) What the violent method invariably does is to awaken the ego which necessarily results in a breakdown of social equilibrium. On the other hand, non-violent activism awakens the conscience. From this results an awakening in people of introspection and self-appraisal. And according to the Qur'an, the miraculous outcome of this is that "he who is your enemy will become your dearest friend." (41:34)

2. A great advantage of the non-violent method is that, by following it, no part of one's time is wasted. The opportunities available in any given situation may then be exploited to the fullest extent—as happened after the no-war pact of Hudaybiya. This peace treaty enabled the energies of the believers to be utilised in peaceful constructive activities instead of being dissipated in a futile armed encounter. One great harm done by violent activism is the breaking of social traditions in the launching of militant movements. Conversely, the great benefit that accrues from non-violent activism is that it can be initiated and prolonged with no damage to tradition.

Generally speaking, attempts to improve or replace existing systems by violent activism are counter-productive. One coup d'état is often the signal for a series of coups and counter-coups, none of which benefit the common man. The truly desirable revolution is that which permits gradual and beneficial changes. And this can be achieved only on the basis of non-violence.

Success Through the Non-violent Method

All the great successes of the first phase of Islam as well as the succeeding periods were achieved by non-violent methods. Listed below are some examples of these successes.

1. Of the 23 year period of prophethood, the initial 13 years were spent by the Prophet in Mecca. The Prophet fully adopted the way of pacifism or non-violence during this time. There were many such issues in Mecca at that time which could have been the subject of clash and confrontation. But, sedulously avoiding all such issues, the Prophet of Islam strictly limited his sphere to peaceful propagation of the word of God. This resulted in *Dawah* work being performed in full force throughout this period. One of the great gains during these 13 years of *dawah* work was the entry into the Islamic fold of men of the highest moral calibre who were responsible for forming the history of Islam, for instance, Abu Bakr, Umar, Usman and Ali, etc.

2. In Mecca when the Quraysh leaders were set to wage war against the Prophet, even then, instead of opting for the way of reaction and retaliation, what the Prophet did was to secretly migrate to Medina.

Migration, by its very nature, was a clear example of non-violent activism. This peaceful strategy enabled the Prophet and his followers, about two hundred in number, to form a powerful centre of Islam in Medina. Had they adopted the path of confrontation instead of peaceful migration, the history of Islam might have been buried right there in Mecca shortly after its inception.

3. After the emigration, his antagonists took the unilateral decision to wage war against him. Consequently such bloody encounters as those of Badr and Uhud took place. Then the Prophet made a 10-year peace treaty known in history as Sulh al-Hudaybiya, by accepting all the conditions of his opponents. This has been called a

'clear victory' in the Qur'an. It is this peace treaty, paving the way for peaceful constructive activities which ultimately made possible the conquest of Mecca and the whole of Arabia.

4. By the end of the pious caliphate, a bloody encounter took place between the Banu Hashim and the Banu Umayya. This stopped the advance of Islam for a period of ten years. What set this process in motion once again was the voluntary withdrawal of Hasan ibn Ali (d. 50 A.H.) from the battlefield. This was undeniably a practical form of non-violent activism. This peaceful move on the part of Hasan ibn Ali re-opened to Islam the locked doors of progress.

5. During the last days of the Abbasid caliphate Mongol tribes attacked the Muslim world and right from Samarkand to Aleppo destroyed the entire Muslim world. The history of Islam had apparently come to a standstill. At that moment the spirit of *dawah* work was born within the Muslims. As a result, the majority of the Mongols converted to Islam. And that miracle took place which has been described by an orientalist in these words: "The religion of Muslims has conquered where their arms had failed."

6. Islamic history took a crucial turn when, in the years succeeding the pious caliphate, rot had set in in the system of the government, and the caliphate had turned into monarchy. At that juncture, many factors emerged which would result in clash and confrontation between the ruler and the ruled. But, following the guidance of the Prophet, the Muslims totally avoided political confrontation. This history beginning with the Umayyad caliphate, continued for several centuries. This was possible because the *tabieen* (companions of the Prophet's companions) and their

succeeding generations, consisting of traditionists, jurists, ulema, sufis and other great religious scholars, all scrupulously avoided any clash or confrontation with the rulers.

It was during this period that peaceful dawah work was started in various countries and the disciplines of hadith, fiqh and other Islamic sciences came into existence on a large scale after a long period of great ideological struggle. All the precious books which adorn our libraries, all the classical literature of Islam are the result of these peaceful activities.

For instance, the hadith as a source of shariah is second only to the Qur'an in Islam. These traditions now exist in the form of printed books. These books are so precious that, without them, it would not have been possible to develop Islam into a complete system as it exists today. During the Umayyads and Abbasids, when the political system had begun to deteriorate, where were these tens of thousands of traditions. All of them existed in the memory of the religious scholars, whose names are mentioned in the books as chains in the link of authorities who have handed this legacy down to us. Had they adopted the principle of violent activism and clashed with the 'oppressive' rulers, they would all have been slaughtered by them and the entire legacy of traditions instead of finding a place on the pages of books, would have been buried along with them in the graveyards. It is by the miracle of having adopted non-violence instead of violence that the precious sources of our traditions have survived in book form and, till today, adorn our libraries.

Political Revolt Unlawful

Despite the blatant perversion in the Muslim rulers after the pious caliphate, the Muslim ulema did not lead an insurrection against these corrupt individuals. For about a period of one thousand years they remained detached in this matter and continued to engage all their efforts in non-material fields. This was not a matter of accident but in obedience to the injunctions of the shariah.

As we know, in the books of hadith detailed traditions have been set down in the chapters titled 'kitabul fitan'. The Prophet of Islam observed in plain words that in later times perversions would set in in the rulers, they would become tyrannical and unjust, but that Muslims should not wield their swords against them. They should rather move to the mountains with their goats and camels.

By 'goats and camels' are meant the opportunities in non-political fields which exist, even when the political institutions are corrupted. This injunction given by the Prophet meant that the Muslims should avail of such opportunities by avoiding clash and confrontation in the political field. In short, by ignoring the political problem, they should avail of the non-political opportunities.

These injunctions of the Prophet of Islam were so clear that the Muslim ulema of later times formed a consensus to make insurrection against the rulers unlawful.

Imam An-Nawawi, commenting upon some traditions as set forth by Sahih Muslim (*Kitab Al-Imarah*) observes: "You should not come into conflict with the rulers in matters of their power. Even if you find them going against express Islamic injunctions, you should attempt to make the truth clear to them solely through words of wisdom and advice. So far as revolt and war against them in order to unseat them is concerned, that is totally unlawful according to the consensus of the ulema, even when the rulers are *zalim* and *fasiq* (tyrants and evil)." (Sahih Muslim, Bisharh An-Nawawi, 12/229)

This command of the Prophet, as clearly expressed
above, was based on extremely important considerations.
In actual fact, in the early phase of Islam (as well as in the
later phase) *dawah* and reform works had to be performed,
without which the history of Islam would not have been
complete. If the ulema of the Muslim community had
tried to pose a threat to the political institutions, certainly
all this constructive work would have been left undone.
That is why the Prophet of Islam expressly prohibited any
clash with political institutions. This avoidance of strife
guaranteed that non-political constructive work would
continue to be performed without any break.

In every society there are always two systems side by
side, one political and the other non-political. The latter is
established through various non-political institutions.
According to the scheme of Islam, non-political institutions
established at the social level have always to remain
stable. In this way there is a continuing endeavour—even
when the political institutions have become corrupt, or
keep changing—to keep Islam firmly established at the
level of the non-political system.

The Command of War in Islam

It is a fact that certain verses in the Qur'an convey the
command to do battle (*qital*) (22:39). What the special
circumstances are which justify the issuance of and
compliance with this command we learn from our study
of the Qur'an.

1. The first point to be noted is that aggression or the
launching of an offensive by the believers is not totally
forbidden. It is permissible, but with certain provisos. We
are clearly commanded in the Qur'an: Fight for the sake of
God those that fight against you, *but do not be aggressive.*
(2:190)

2. Only defensive war is permitted in Islam. Such a war is one in which aggression is committed by some other party so that the believers have to fight in self-defence. Initiating hostility is not permitted for Muslims. The Qur'an says: "They were the first to attack you." (9:13)

Furthermore, even in the case of the offensive being launched by an opposing group, the believers are not supposed to retaliate immediately. Rather in the beginning all efforts are to be made to avert war, and only when avoidance has become impossible is battle to be resorted to inevitably in defence.

3. According to the Qur'an there was one form of war which was time-bound strictly in relation to its purpose. This was to put an end to *fitna* 'Fight against them until *fitna* is no more.' (2:193) In this verse *fitna* signifies that coercive system which had reached the extremes of religious persecution. In ancient times this coercive political system prevailed all over the world. This absolutism had closed all the doors of progress, both spiritual and material. At that time God commanded the believers to break this coercive system in order to usher in freedom, so that all doors of spiritual and material progress might be opened to man.

This mission was undertaken and brought to a successful conclusion at the internal level within Arabia during the life of the Prophet. Later, during the pious caliphate, the Sasanid and Byzantine empires were dismantled with special divine succour. Consequently, intellectual oppression at the international level was replaced by intellectual freedom.

In this connection those traditions are worth noting which are enshrined in Sahih al-Bukhari. When, after the fourth caliph Ali ibn Abi Talib, political conflict ensued between Abdullah ibn Zubayr and the Umayyads, Abdullah ibn Umar, the seniormost companion of the Prophet held himself aloof from the battle. People approached him and, quoting the verse of *qital-e-fitna*, asked him why he was not joining in the battle. Abdullah ibn Umar replied that *'fitna'* as mentioned in the Qur'an did not refer to political infighting, but rather to the religious coercive system, that had already been put to an end by them. (Fathul Bari, 8/60)

From this we learn that the war against *fitna* was a war of limited duration, meant to be engaged in only until its specific purpose had been served.

Invoking the Quranic exhortation to do battle against *fitna* in order to validate acts of war which had quite other aims was improper. This verse could be cited only if the same state of affairs as existed at the time of its revelation, were to prevail once again.

The biographers of the Prophet of Islam have put the number of *ghazwa* (battle) at more than 80. This gives the impression that the Prophet of Islam in his 23-year prophetic career waged about four battles in a year. But this impression is entirely baseless. The truth is that the Prophet of Islam in his entire prophetic life, engaged in war only on three occasions. All the other incidents described as *ghazwa* were in actual fact examples of avoidance of war and not instances of involvement in battle.

For instance, in the books of seerah, the incident of Al-Ahzab is called a *ghazwa* (battle), whereas the truth is that on this occasion the armed tribes of Arabia, twelve thousand in number, reached the borders of Medina with all intentions of waging war, but the Prophet and his companions dug a deep trench between them, thus successfully preventing a battle from taking place. The same is the case with all the other incidents called *ghazwa*. The opponents of the Prophet repeatedly tried to get him embroiled in war, but on all such occasions, he managed to resort to some such strategy as averted the war, thus defusing the situation.

There were only three instances of Muslims really entering the field of battle—Badr, Uhud and Hunayn. But the events tell us that on all these occasions, war had become inevitable, so that the Prophet was compelled to encounter the aggressors in self-defence. Furthermore, these battles lasted only for half a day, each beginning from noon and ending with the setting of the sun. Thus it would be proper to say that the Prophet in his entire life span had actively engaged in war for a total of a day and a half. That is to say, the Prophet had observed the principle of non-violence throughout his 23-year prophetic career, except for one and a half days.

The Islamic method, being based totally on the principle of non-violence, it is unlawful for believers to initiate hostilities. Except in cases where self-defence has become inevitable, the Qur'an in no circumstance gives permission for violence.

The Modern Age and Non-Violence

The greatest problem facing Islam today is, as I see it, that Muslims have almost totally forgotten the *sunnah* (Prophet's way) of non-violence. In latter times when the Ottoman and Mughal empires disintegrated and problems like that of Palestine have had to be confronted by the faithful, Muslims all over the world have fallen a prey to negative reaction on a colossal scale; they have failed to remember that the policy of Islam is not that of violence but of non-violence. It is the result of this deviation, that despite almost a 100-years of bloody wars, Muslims have achieved no positive gain. Rather whatever they already had has been lost by them.

According to Imam Malik, later generations of this ummah (Muslim community) settled matters at issue in the same way that earlier generations had done, i.e. non-violent methods. Similarly, Muslims of modern times must likewise resort only to non-violent methods. Just as no gain could accrue from violent methods earlier, no gain can accrue from violent methods today.

The state of affairs of Muslims in modern times resembles that which prevailed at the time of Hudaybiya. Today once again—only on a far larger scale—this *hamiyat al-jahiliya* prejudices prevailing in pre-Islamic Arabia (48:28) is being displayed by the other party. In the first phase of Islam its solution lay in Muslims sedulously avoiding an equivalent display of prejudice, and in holding firmly *kalema at-taqwa* they became entitled to the succour of God and were granted a clear victory (48:26).

At the time of the Hudaybiya peace treaty, the Quraysh, who had secured the leadership of Arabia, were bent on waging war. The Kaaba was in their possession. They had expelled the Prophet and his companions from their home town. They had taken possession of Muslims' homes and other properties, and spared no effort in disseminating negative propaganda against Islam.

Given this state of affairs, there were only two options before the believers. One was to attempt to put an end to tyranny and launch an outright war on the other party in the name of securing their rights. The result of such a move would certainly have been further loss in terms of lives and property.

The second option was to remain patient in the face of immediate loss, be it political or material, and, in spite of the losses avail of whatever opportunities are already available. The Prophet of Islam and his companions chose this second course. The result was that in just a few years time the entire history of Arabia was altered for the better by an Islamic revolution.

The same state of affairs is widespread in modern times. Although today Muslims have suffered great losses, political and material, at the hands of other nations, there still exist a great number of opportunities only for self-betterment and for *dawah* work on a far larger scale. If availed of wisely, we can rewrite the history of Islam in magnificent terms.

The Manifestation of Religion

The aim of the revolution brought about by the Prophet and his companions in the seventh century is stated in the Qur'an to be *izhar-e-deen*. (*Izhar* in Arabic means dominance/ascendancy/supremacy. Here *izhar-e-deen* signifies intellectual and ideological dominance, not political dominance. This means that in intellectual and ideological respects, God's religion assumes ascendancy over all other ideologies and religions.)

Izhar-e-deen was not an incident of short duration, but an ongoing assertion of the eternal dominance of Islam. Its implication was that in the world of ideology, such a revolution would be brought about as would establish the supremacy of Islam forever. Its purpose was to unravel all the veils of superstition which clouded human judgement, and to lay bare the scientific proofs hidden in nature, so that the truth of monotheism could be brought to light for all humanity. As the Qur'an puts it, 'They desire to extinguish the light of Allah with their mouths: but Allah seeks only to perfect His light, however much the infidels may abhor it.' (9:32, 33)

Granting ideological ascendancy to God's religion was a matter of considerable complexity, amounting to the writing of history afresh. For although God's unassailable truth had always existed, it had become obscured by false and misguided ideas, because thinking, the arts and learning in general had all become fettered by superstition and idolatry. This had led to a veil being thrown over true religion, which was the only proper vehicle for God's truth. The coercive systems of the monarchies which prevailed all over the world at that time were responsible for perpetuating this state of affairs, for any intellectual freedom, particularly the freedom of religion, would have been a challenge to their supreme authority. Under such systems, there could be only such social development as suited individual rulers, and there could be no scientific development whatsoever.

Systems of governance which depended on religious persecution had, therefore, to be overthrown, so that a propitious atmosphere could be created for the performance of *dawah* of the true religion. This was carried into effect with resounding success by the Prophet and his companions, and all arguments were rallied in support of God's true religion, so that all other religions would be divested of their former influence. This abolition of oppressive systems and the freeing of people's minds from superstition naturally led to free scientific enquiry, a process which Islam has continued to foster over the centuries without interruption, and which has culminated in the unparalleled scientific achievements of the present day.

The technological advance which have been made possible by this scientific revolution have in turn provided Islam with an improved means of propagating Islam, namely modern communications. By making use of the media, those engaged in *dawah* work can spread the word of God much further and much faster than ever before. According to a hadith, a time was to come when God's word would enter all the homes in the world. (*Musnad*, Ahmad). This was indirectly a prediction of the advent of our modern age of communications.

In ancient times, the study of religion could be done only as something sacred and as a matter of dogma. That is why established and unestablished religions had not, academically been distinguished from one another. In modern times, thanks to the influence of the scientific revolution, the study of religions can be done as objectively and as critically as any other matter which comes under scientific scrutiny. Such critical study has proved, purely academically, that historically there is only one reliable religion, and that is Islam. All other religions are lacking in this historical credibility. Prior to this, the *dayees* of Islam could resort only to traditional arguments in support of their faith, but it has become possible to measure up Islamic realities by the highest standards of human knowledge and to establish its authenticity by purely logical arguments. Indeed, in latter times, the sciences themselves have born out the divine truths of Islam.

Yet, despite modern developments, our own times are constantly regarded as being fraught with problems for Islam. Muslims, lacking in understanding and awareness, forget that the modern age has never ceased to be the age of Islam. They fail to appreciate that Islam's potential remains undiminished, and that it is for believers to convert that potential into an immediate reality. They should take into account the fact that, in the wake of the scientific revolution, which is itself the direct outcome of the Islamic revolution, it has become possible to begin a serious and beneficial dialogue between Islam and non-Islam, the result of which will necessarily be in favour of Islam. Now, this being so, the need of the hour is for Muslims to put an end unilaterally to all violent activities against *madu* (addressee) nations, so that a normal, amicable relationship may be allowed to grow between *dayee* and *madu*.

A Great Opportunity

1. Since direct argument cannot be applied to religious beliefs pertaining to the unseen world, these can be supported only by indirect or inferential argument. Educated people had therefore come to believe that religious realities belonged only to the domain of dogma, and that they were not academic or scientific realities. But after the breaking up of the atom the science of logic has undergone a change, and it has been accepted that inferential argument too, in its nature, is as valid and reliable as direct argument. It has subsequently become possible for religious realities to be established on an academic level, i.e. exactly on the same level as material or non-religious theories.

2. In ancient times when man observed the world, it appeared to him that in nature there existed things which were very different from one another. This observation of appearance produced the mentality of idolatry. People began to think that in view of the great diversity of things in existence, their Creator too would perforce take many and varied shapes. But scientific study has shown that this

variety is only that of appearance. Otherwise, all things in nature are different expressions of the same matter. In this way *shirk* (idolatry) came to be seen as an intellectually untenable practice, while monotheism gained the solid support of logic.

3. According to a statement of the Qur'an, the signs of God lay hidden in the earth and the heavens. The study of science has made it manifest to all men that the universe is a great storehouse of divine arguments. "We will show them Our signs in all the regions of the earth and in their own souls, until they clearly see that this is the Truth." (41:53)

4. After the new discoveries of science, many such things have come to the knowledge of man as have rendered it possible to prove with new arguments those events which are of important religious significance. For instance, carbon 14 dating has made it possible to determine the exact age of the mummy of Rameses II, thereby providing scientific proof for the statement of the Qur'an that the body of Pharaoh was saved by God, so that it might become "a sign to all posterity." (10:92)

Islam in the Present Age

Now the question arises as to whether an Islam which teaches non-violence can be of relevance in the present age, and assume a superior position once again in new situations.

The answer is entirely in the positive. The truth is that Islam's being a peaceful religion shows that it is an eternal religion. Had it been a religion of violence, it would not have been eternal. For, in modern times, the way of violence has been totally rejected by contemporary thinking. Now only that system is worthy of consideration and acceptance the teachings of which are based on peace and non-violence.

Modern thinking, for example, has rejected communism. One of the major reasons was that communism had to be sustained by violence. And under no circumstances is violence acceptable to the modern mind. Nazism and Fascism too have been rejected on similar grounds. Modern man, therefore, disapproves of religious and non-religious extremism, because they lead man, willy nilly, to violence.

But Islam is a religion of nature. It has held violence as inadmissible from the outset. Islam has been an upholder of peace, not violence, from day one.

In the past, Islam played a great role in the development of humanity, as a result of which human history entered a new age of progress and development. The time has come today for Islam to play a great constructive role, leading human history once again into a new age of progress.

What is called scientific or technical progress is the result of the discovery of some of the great secrets of nature. But if nature and its mysteries have always existed in our world, why has there been such a long delay in their discovery? Why could not the scientific advancement of the last few hundred years have been made thousands of years ago?

The reason was that in ancient times scientific enquiry was anathema to men of religion, to the point where religious persecution had become an inseparable obstacle to the progress of science. Since ancient times, religion and science (divine knowledge and human knowledge) were linked with one another. What Islam did was separate religion (which had become, in essence, a set of irrational beliefs) from scientific research and investigation. For instance, eclipses of the sun and moon had been linked with human destiny. The Prophet of Islam declared that eclipses had nothing to do with the lot of human beings. These were astronomical events, not events pertaining to the fate of mankind. (*Fathul Bari,* 2/611)

The incident of the pollination of dates is recorded in the books of hadith. The Prophet of Islam observed that in worldly matters such as these, "you should act according to your experience, as you know these matters better." (Sahih Muslim Bi Sharh An-Nawawi, 15/117)

This meant delinking religion and science from one another. In this way scientific research acquired an atmosphere of freedom for its functioning. For the first time in human history science (human knowledge) could be developed freely without the intervention of religion. And advancing gradually, culminated in the attainment of the modern age.

But, today man is again facing an even greater problem. That is, despite the extraordinary progress made in the field of science and technology, human beings are confronted with the problem of not knowing the limit of freedom.

Modern man aspired to freedom as the highest good, but once having reached this goal, he was unable to set reasonable limits to freedom. In consequence, unrestrained freedom descended into anarchy and lawlessness. This is the actual cause of many of the problems which are emerging in modern times in western society. Now man requires an ideology which delimits his freedom, drawing the line between desirable and undesirable freedom. And it is only Islam which can provide him with such an ideology.

Now is the time for this ideology to be presented to

man, who is ready and waiting to accept it.

After the fall of communism (1991), much of the world was and still is, faced with an ideological vacuum. This vacuum can be filled by Islam alone. In the present world the developed countries have become economic or military superpowers, but the place is vacant for an ideological superpower, and that, potentially belongs to Islam.

There is only one obstacle in converting a great potential into a reality in favour of Islam. And that is the repeated recourse to violence by Muslim movements in modern times. Such action has presented Islam before the world in the guise of a violent religion. For this reason the man of today shies away from Islam. He fails to study Islam objectively. If this barrier could be removed and Islam once again brought before the world as a non-violent religion, or as a peaceful social system, then once again humanity would accept it, recognising it to be the voice of its own nature.

Modern man is in need of a new religion or a new system, based on peace. It should be free from superstitious beliefs, and should provide the answers to deep psychological questions, on our flawed existence. Its principles should not clash with scientific realities, and it should be supported by a victorious history.

Today no religion but Islam can lay such positive claims to acceptance, for it is Islam and Islam alone which fulfills all these conditions. Individually, there are many men and women today who, after having studied Islam, have acknowledged these unique qualities in Islam. Some have acknowledged them in theory while others have gone ahead and accepted Islam in practice.

Dawah Activism

Islamic activism in respect of its method is based on non-violence and in respect of its target is based on *dawah*. *Dawah*, in fact, is another name for a peaceful struggle for the propagation of Islam. It would be true to say that Islamic activism in fact is *dawah* activism.

The task of *dawah* is no simple one. It enjoys the status of a key factor. If this task is fully performed, all other objectives will be automatically achieved. Here are certain references from the Qur'an in this connection.

1. Through *dawah* the believers receive God's protection against the mischief of the opponents.

2. Through *dawah* even the direst of enemies turns into a dearest friend. (41:34)

3. *Dawah* proves Islam's ideological superiority. And without doubt nothing is greater than the superiority of ideology. (10:32)

4. Through *dawah* a positive mentality is inculcated within the *ummah*. This is called 'honest counsel' in the Qur'an. (7:68)

5. The mission of *dawah* is performed by human beings but the conducive conditions for it are provided by God. Just as the farming is to be done by the farmer while the rains come from God. In modern times favourable conditions have been fully provided to man. Now the believers' duty is to refrain from expending their energies in futile activities. They must exert their entire energy in *dawah* work. All the best results will ensue from this act.

6. The Prophet of Islam along with about two hundred of his companions left Mecca when the Meccan leaders had made it impossible for them to stay there. The Meccans had even decided to kill the Prophet. But the first

speech the Prophet made on reaching Medina had no taste
of bitterness, neither did it contain any mention of
vengeance on or violence against the Quraysh.

On reaching Medina first priority was given to the task
of entering into peace treaties with the tribes in and
around Medina, for instance with the Banu Khuza'a, etc.
According to their pact neither would they fight against
the Muslims nor would the Muslims fight against them.
Most of the tribes in Arabia joined in these truce
agreements.

But the Quraysh did not desist from aggression, and
even engaged in certain military forays against the
Muslims. But, finally, in the sixth year of Hijrah, the
Prophet succeeded in making a peace treaty with the
Quraysh as well at a place called Hudaybiya, albeit on
acceptance of all the conditions laid down by the Quraysh.

Muslims Displaced

It is an incontrovertible fact that Muslims have not
been able to join the mainstream in modern times. At all
places and in every department they are leading their
lives as if driven into a corner. This is undoubtedly an
extremely critical problem, for it has relegated Muslims to
second class positions all over the world.

To me, the greatest reason for this is the violent
attitude of the Muslims. Today's Muslims are easily
provoked and become violent at anything which is against
their way of thinking, or even not to their liking. It is true
that not all Muslims become involved in acts of violence.
Yet all Muslims would be regarded involved in this
matter. This is because that section, of Muslims—in fact,
the majority—who are not personally involved, neither
disown those members of their community who are

engaged in violence, nor even condemn them. In such a case, according to the Islamic shariah itself if the involved Muslims are directly responsible, the uninvolved Muslims are also indirectly responsible.

It is Muslims' religious and secular leaders who are actually responsible for this violent approach on the part of Muslims today. In modern times when Muslims have had to undergo the experience of defeat, almost all the religious, secular scholars (*ulama*) and intellectuals follow one single line, that of awakening the spirit of *jihad* (in the sense of *qital*) among Muslims. The entire Muslim world reverberates with such slogans as 'Jihad is our way and Jihad is the only solution to our problems!'

The entire world has witnessed a great number of large and small movements in violent response to the problems faced by Muslims.

If you go to Palestine, you will hear the youth singing a song no doubt taught to them by their elders:

Let's make war, let's make war,

For war is the way to success.

In modern times the violent approach of our ulema, intellectuals, and leaders of movements, is the sole reason for the present violent mentality among Muslims all over the world. It is as a result of this mentality that, if anyone writes a book against Islam, Muslims are prepared to kill the writer. If any procession raises anti-Muslim slogans, Muslims start stoning the procession instead of killing the evil by observing silence, which, as Umar Faruq advocated, would be the best strategy in this case. If there is any monetary or territorial controversy with any nation, they immediately take up arms against it, rather than adopt a peaceful strategy to solve the problem.

This violent mentality of Muslims is responsible for

having alienated them from their neighbours everywhere. Their conduct clearly shows that they no longer cherish the ideal of universal brotherhood. Everywhere they are looked upon with aversion and dread. One can even see notices on walls which say 'Beware of Muslims', instead of 'Beware of dogs.' And if these words are not inscribed on walls, they are certainly inscribed on the hearts and minds of the people. The resulting dissociation has left Muslims a backward group in modern times. Even in advanced countries like America they remain backward as a community in comparison with other immigrant groups.

The only way to alleviate the tragic plight of Muslims is to bring them back to non-violent Islam, by helping to understand that their violent version of Islam is not the true one.

As soon as Muslims take to the path of non-violent Islam, they will be able to become equal partners with other communities. They will have joined the universal mainstream, and will consequently be able to participate in all activities, in all institutions. People instead of dreading them, will welcome then in very field them. They will become a part of the universal brotherhood. Their issues will be looked upon with justice. Their equal partnership will be certain in all institutions ranging from the social to the educational.

Peaceful interaction will give Muslims the kind of intellectual stimulation and variety of experience which they must have if they are to tread the path of progress.

Interaction will also facilitate the task of *dawah* on a large scale. The natural result of this vast interaction of Muslims and non-Muslims will be that everywhere dialogue on Islam will be started, formally as well as informally. In modern times, because of the extremist and violent attitude of Muslims, serious dialogue between Islam and non-Islam has almost come to an end. Now when peaceful interaction between Muslims and non-Muslims takes place in a normal atmosphere, serious dialogue will ensue on its own. The beginning of serious dialogue between Islam and non-Islam is, without doubt, a very great success from the point of view of *dawah*.

The Qur'an describes Sulh Al-Hudaybiya, in the early period of Islam as a 'clear victory'. It was a 'clear victory' in the sense that it established peace between the believers in *tawhid* and believers in *shirk*, thus making it possible for a serious dialogue to be held between the two on religious matters.

In modern times if Muslims abandon the path of violence and fully adopt the path of non-violence, this will be for Muslims like reviving the sunnah of Hudaybiya. And they will start receiving those great benefits which Islam and Muslims had gained after the event of Hudaybiya in the first phase.

Peace and Justice

One great problem for Muslims is that peace does not necessarily guarantee them justice. This has caused Muslims to become violent and to neglect opportunities for *dawah*. In modern times Muslims want a peace which brings them justice. But according to the law of nature, this kind of peace can never be achieved, that is why Muslims the world over are in a state of physical and mental unrest. Distressed in their minds, they have become violent in their thinking and in their actions.

The truth is that peace does not automatically produce justice. Peace in actual fact simply opens up opportunities for the achievement of justice. At the time of Hudaybiya the Prophet of Islam had not found justice. He had achieved peace but only by delinking it from justice. The Prophet had made this peace not to exact justice but to receive the opportunities. And great opportunities for *dawah* action did open up with the establishment of peace. The Prophet exploited these opportunities in full measure. Therefore, in just a few years' time the Prophet not only ensured justice, but set Islam upon a much more solid footing.

The Muslims of the present day have to understand this secret of nature. Only then will it be possible for them first to find peace, then ultimately their desired goal of justice.

Conclusion

In October 1997, I met a 36-year old European, Leon Zippo Hayes, who was born in the city of Christchurch in New Zealand. After having studied Islam, he has changed his religion. His Islamic name is Khalilur Rahman. Passing through Muslim countries he is going to perform Hajj by land.

During the conversation he said that in modern times Muslims are engaged in bloody war at many places, at some places with others and at other places among themselves. This had led him (like many others) to conclude that perhaps Islam was a religion of violence. Later, he studied the Qur'an with the help of translations, and when he reached this verse in the Qur'an: 'Whoever killed a human being should be looked upon as though he had killed all mankind (5:32),' he said that he was so moved that he could not believe that it was in the Qur'an.

This incident is broadly indicative of the thinking of non-Muslims on Islam. On seeing the actions of Muslims, people today find it hard to believe that Islam may be a religion of peace. But if Muslims stop engaging in violent activities and give people the opportunity to appreciate Islam in its original form, then certainly a great number of people would realise as they never had before that Islam was a peaceful religion and they would rush to it, saying and that it was exactly the religion which their souls had been seeking all along.

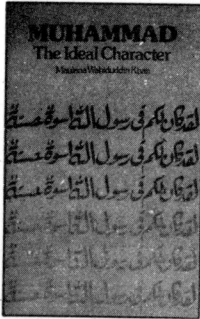
MUHAMMAD
The Ideal Character
Maulana Wahiduddin Khan

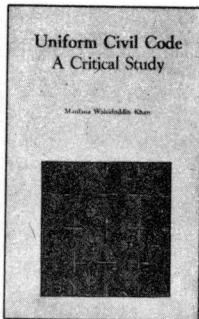
Uniform Civil Code
A Critical Study
Maulana Wahiduddin Khan

ISLAM
The Voice of
Human Nature
Maulana Wahiduddin Khan

Polygamy
and
Islam

Tabligh Movement

ISLAM
AS IT IS
Maulana Wahiduddin Khan

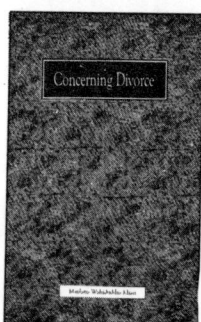
Concerning Divorce
Maulana Wahiduddin Khan

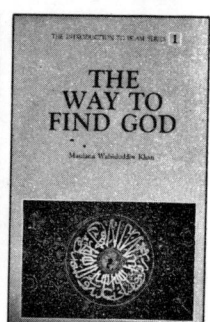
THE INTRODUCTION TO ISLAM SERIES 1
THE WAY TO FIND GOD
Maulana Wahiduddin Khan

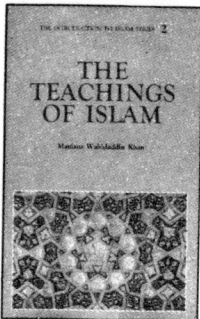
THE INTRODUCTION TO ISLAM SERIES 2
THE TEACHINGS OF ISLAM
Maulana Wahiduddin Khan

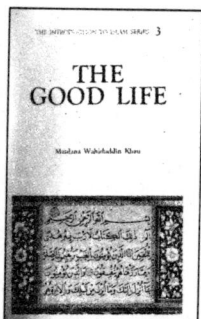
THE INTRODUCTION TO ISLAM SERIES 3
THE GOOD LIFE
Maulana Wahiduddin Khan

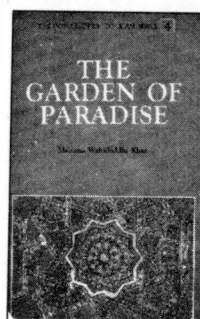
THE INTRODUCTION TO ISLAM SERIES 4
THE GARDEN OF PARADISE
Maulana Wahiduddin Khan

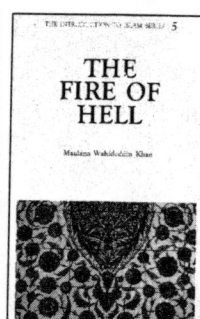
THE INTRODUCTION TO ISLAM SERIES 5
THE FIRE OF HELL
Maulana Wahiduddin Khan

रास्ते
बन्द नहीं
मौलाना वहीदुद्दीन ख़ान

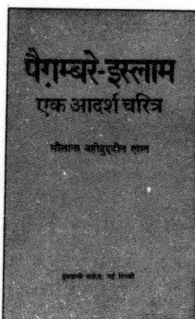
पैग़म्बरे-इस्लाम
एक आदर्श चरित्र
मौलाना वहीदुद्दीन ख़ान
इस्लामी सेंटर, नई दिल्ली

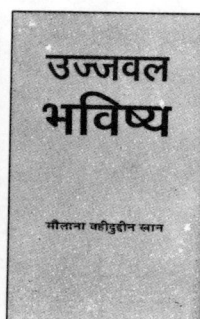
उज्जवल
भविष्य
मौलाना वहीदुद्दीन ख़ान

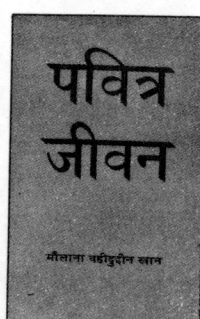
पवित्र
जीवन
मौलाना वहीदुद्दीन ख़ान

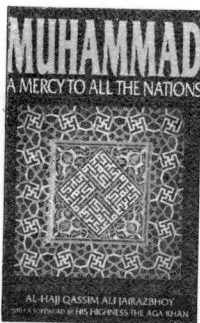
MUHAMMAD
A MERCY TO ALL THE NATIONS
AL-HAJJ QASSIM ALI JAIRAZBHOY
WITH A FOREWORD BY HIS HIGHNESS THE AGA KHAN

Heart of the Koran
Lex Hixon

The Soul of the Qur'an
INSPIRING PRAYERS TO KINDLE HEART AND MIND
SANIYASNAIN KHAN

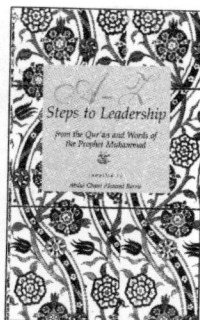
Steps to Leadership
from the Qur'an and Words of the Prophet Muhammad
compiled by Abdul Ghani Hamood Barcia

The Muslim Marriage Guide
Ruqaiyyah Waris Maqsood

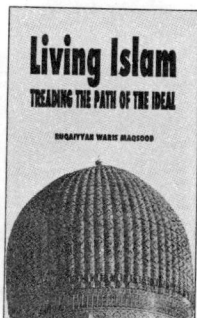
Living Islam
TREADING THE PATH OF THE IDEAL
RUQAIYYAH WARIS MAQSOOD

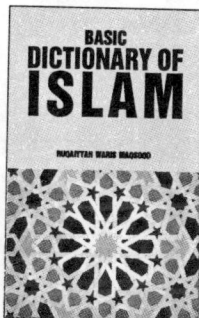
BASIC DICTIONARY OF ISLAM
RUQAIYYAH WARIS MAQSOOD

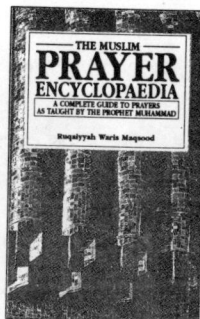
THE MUSLIM PRAYER ENCYCLOPAEDIA
A COMPLETE GUIDE TO PRAYERS AS TAUGHT BY THE PROPHET MUHAMMAD
Ruqaiyyah Waris Maqsood

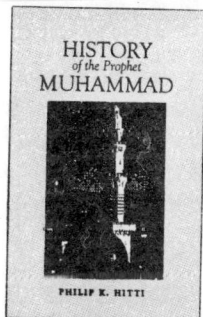
HISTORY of the Prophet MUHAMMAD
PHILIP K. HITTI

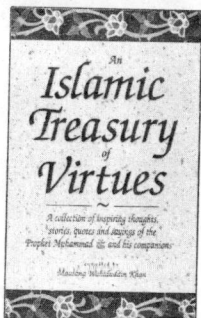
An Islamic Treasury of Virtues
A collection of inspiring thoughts, stories, quotes and sayings of the Prophet Muhammad ﷺ and his companions
compiled by Maulana Wahiduddin Khan

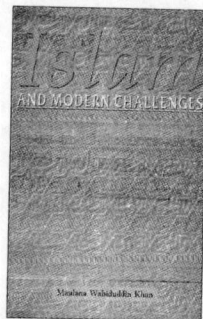
Islam AND MODERN CHALLENGES
Maulana Wahiduddin Khan

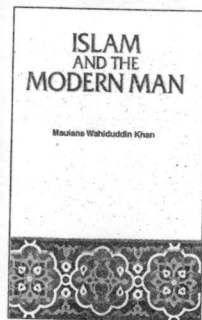
ISLAM AND THE MODERN MAN
Maulana Wahiduddin Khan

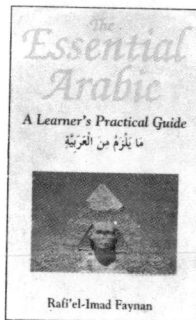
The Essential Arabic
A Learner's Practical Guide
ما يَلزَم من العَرَبِيَّة
Rafi'el-Imad Faynan

THE HOLY QUR'AN
TRANSLATION AND COMMENTARY BY ABDULLAH YUSUF ALI

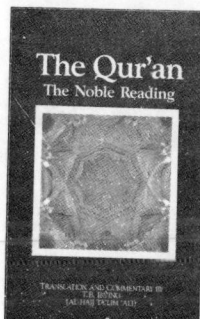
The Qur'an
The Noble Reading
TRANSLATION AND COMMENTARY BY T.B. IRVING
AL-HAJJ TA'LIM ALI

The Qur'an
TRANSLATION
القرآن الحكيم

MUHAMMAD
A PROPHET FOR ALL HUMANITY

MAULANA WAHIDUDDIN KHAN

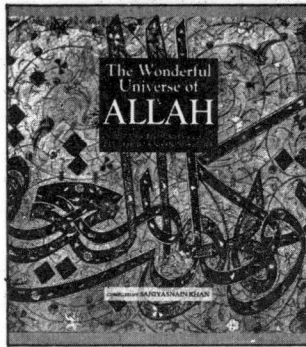

The Wonderful
Universe of
ALLAH

Translation SANIYASNAIN KHAN

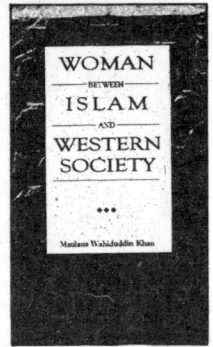

WOMAN
BETWEEN
ISLAM
AND
WESTERN
SOCIETY

Maulana Wahiduddin Khan

QURANIC WISDOM FOR MODERN LIVING

PRESENTING
THE QUR'ĀN

A BRIEF INTRODUCTION TO ALL THE
114 CHAPTERS OF THE QUR'ĀN

SANIYASNAIN KHAN

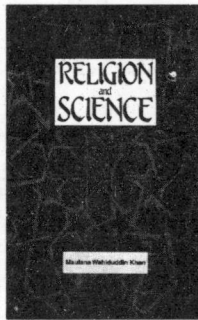

RELIGION
and
SCIENCE

Maulana Wahiduddin Khan

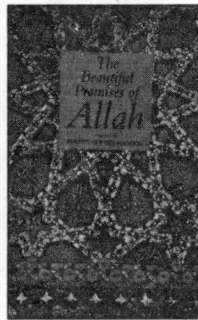

The
Beautiful
Promises of
Allah

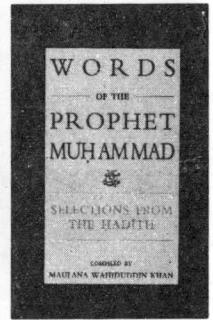

WORDS
OF THE
PROPHET
MUHAMMAD

SELECTIONS FROM
THE HADITH

COMPILED BY
MAULANA WAHIDUDDIN KHAN

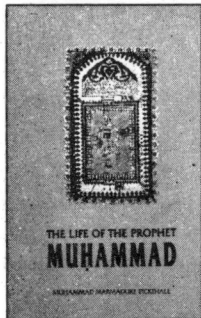

THE LIFE OF THE PROPHET
MUHAMMAD

MUHAMMAD MARMADUKE PICKTHALL

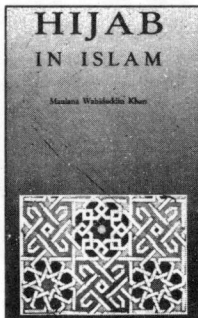

HIJAB
IN ISLAM

Maulana Wahiduddin Khan

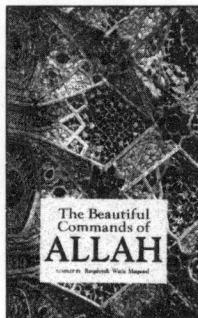

The Beautiful
Commands of
ALLAH

COMPILED BY Rampbrook Waris Maqsood

WOMAN
IN ISLAMIC SHARI'AH

Maulana Wahiduddin Khan

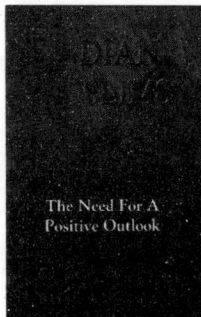

The Need For A
Positive Outlook

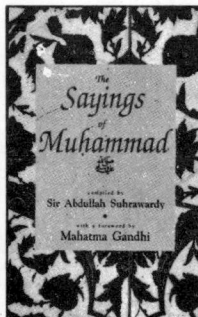

The
Sayings
of
Muhammad

compiled by
Sir Abdullah Suhrawardy

with a foreword by
Mahatma Gandhi

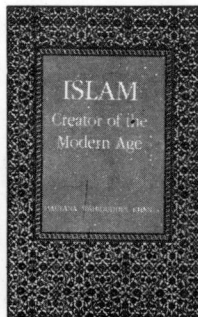

ISLAM
Creator of the
Modern Age

MAULANA WAHIDUDDIN KHAN

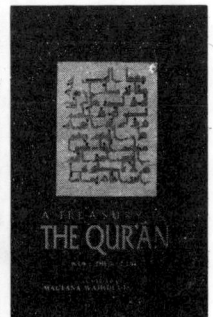

A TREASURY OF
THE QUR'ĀN

MAULANA WAHIDUDDIN KHAN